CONTENTS

Introduction	6
Metrication	8
Beginnings	9
Family Main Dishes:	
Beef	20
Lamb	32
Liver	38
Pork and Bacon	40
Sausagemeat	49
Turkey	52
Chicken	54
Eggs	67
Fish	72
Salads and Vegetables	75
Puddings:	
Cold	90
Hot	105
Home Baking	115
Preserves for the Larder Shelf	131
Christmas Comes Every Year	139
Index	147

Introduction

Cooking has always been a source of fascination to me. My series on 'Good Afternoon' gives me a splendid chance to communicate some of my delight to a very large number of people, for I am told that the programme is watched by over four million people. I cannot possibly know each viewer individually, so I like to imagine that you have the same attitude to cooking that I have. I believe that we all want to produce meals that are good and nutritious to eat, that the preparation should not demand too much time, and that the ingredients used should not be costly. In order to achieve this I discuss the recipes with Judith Chalmers, my other half on the programme; we pool our knowledge and keep our minds open to new ideas – and thoroughly enjoy ourselves in the process. We both hope that this book will help you too to derive pleasure from your cookery, and not regard it as a dreary but necessary daily chore.

This book includes all the recipes that I have shown on 'Good Afternoon' plus more that I shall do in the future. The dishes are fairly classic, made as simple as possible to keep time and expense to a minimum. I have not hesitated to use canned or frozen ingredients where these save time and do not add to the cost. In addition, at the end of each recipe, I have included a cook's tip on how to make things even simpler and more economical, and I have also provided general hints which may be useful to people who are seriously concerned to cut down time and money. The

Mary Berry was born in Bath and studied cooking both there and in Paris. She now lives at Penn in Buckinghamshire with her husband and three young children and combines looking after her family with her cooking on 'Good Afternoon'. She is also cooking consultant to *Home and Freezer Digest Magazine*. She is the author of several books on cooking including *The All Colour Cook Book*, *Popular Freezer Cookery*, *Popular French Cookery* and *The Complete Book of Freezer Cooking*. Mary Berry has been cookery editor of various magazines including *Ideal Home* and *Housewife*. She made her first appearance on 'Good Afternoon' in January 1973 and since then has presented many recipes on the programme.

The front cover illustration shows Mary Berry with Judith Chalmers in the 'Good Afternoon' studio.

good afternoon cookbook

MARY BERRY

SPHERE BOOKS LIMITED
30/32 Gray's Inn Road, London WC1X 8JL

First published in Great Britain by
Sphere Books Ltd 1976
Copyright © Thames Television 1976

Illustrations: Keith Russel

TRADE
MARK

This book is sold subject to the condition that
it shall not, by way of trade or otherwise, be lent,
re-sold, hired out or otherwise circulated without
the publisher's prior consent in any form of
binding or cover other than that in which it is
published and without a similar condition
including this condition being imposed on the
subsequent purchaser.

Set in Monotype Scotch Roman

Printed in Great Britain by
Hazell Watson & Viney Ltd
Aylesbury, Bucks

secret here is to plan ahead. For instance, when you are making a Victoria sandwich, prepare double quantities and use the extra as the basis for a pudding. When you are providing a cheese sauce for cauliflower, make an extra amount and save time later in the week when you come to serve macaroni cheese or lasagne. Save fuel by cooking a whole meal on the top of the stove or, when you are baking, by filling the oven with dishes to be used later. You can make the biggest saving of all by buying food that is in season, when it is at its best and relatively cheap. My 'Good Afternoon' programmes always follow the previous Friday's 'Money-go-Round', in which Tony Bastable and Joan Shenton pick out good food buys, and I watch these very carefully. You can also keep in touch with good buys by listening to local radio and reading local newspapers.

I myself have learnt a great deal from 'Good Afternoon'. It has taught me the satisfaction of careful planning, and has made me extremely practical in all my methods. Each programme lasts only half an hour, so I have to be absolutely sure that the recipes will work out quickly and efficiently: if they don't, viewers soon write to tell me!

So here are my recipes for you to enjoy. One final tip – be adventurous with your cooking, that is part of the fun.

MARY BERRY

METRICATION

The exact conversion from Imperial to metric measures does not usually give very convenient working quantities, so where possible round off the metric measures into units of 25 grammes (e.g. 1 oz – 25 g). However where the proportion between liquids and solids is critical, such as in baking recipes, a more accurate conversion is necessary and you should refer to the table below.

Weight

1 oz – 28·35 g	1 kilogramme – 1000 g –	2 lb 3 oz approx
2 oz – 56·7 g	500 g –	1 lb 1½ oz ,,
4 oz – 113·4 g	250 g –	9 oz ,,
8 oz – 226·8 g	125 g –	4¼ oz ,,
12 oz – 340·2 g	100 g –	3½ oz ,,
16 oz – 453·6 g	25 g –	1 oz ,,

Liquids

¼ pt (1 gill) –	142 ml	
½ pt –	284 ml	
1 pt –	568 ml	
1 litre –	1000 g – 1¾ pt – 35 fl. oz	approx
½ litre –	500 g – ¾ pt plus 4½ tablespoons	,,
¼ litre –	250 g – ½ pt less 2 tablespoons	,,
1 decilitre –	100 g – 6 tablespoons	,,
1 centilitre –	10 g – 1 dessertspoon	,,
1 millilitre –	1 g – a few drops	,,
5 millilitres –	5 g – pharmaceutical teaspoon	,,

Temperatures

Electricity and Solid Fuel	Gas	Degrees Fahrenheit	Centigrade
Cool	¼–½	250	121
Very slow	1	275	135
Slow	2	300	149
	3	325	163
Moderate	4	350	177
	5	375	190
Moderately hot	6	400	205
Hot	7	425	218
Very hot	8	450	232
	9	475	246

beginnings

Stocks

Good home-made stock is a perfect basis for most soups and it is not difficult to make. The best bones to use are beef, veal or chicken. To make a good brown stock, take 3 lbs of beef bones, ideally brown them in the oven while the joint is roasting on Sunday. This will help give the stock a good flavour and colour. Then put them in a large pan and cover with water. For every 2 pints of water, add 1 teaspoon of salt, a few vegetables such as a large onion, two carrots, outside sticks of celery. Do not add strong flavoured vegetables like swede or turnip or starchy vegetables like potatoes. Add a bunch of mixed herbs or $\frac{1}{4}$ teaspoon of dried herbs and simmer gently for four to five hours. Leave overnight to cool. Next day, skim off fat, keep in refrigerator and reboil every two days. If you have a freezer, stock keeps very well and is useful to have on hand. I find it best to reduce the stock and then freeze it in the form of ice cubes.

Stock cubes and water are a very good alternative to home-made stock. Take special care with the amount of salt used in recipes as they are inclined to be rather salty. Chicken stock cubes are milder than beef.

Beetroot Soup
(for six)

1 oz butter
1 medium sized onion, chopped
$\frac{3}{4}$ lb cooked beetroot, skinned and diced
2 pints home-made beef stock *or*
2 beef stock cubes dissolved in
2 pints water
about $\frac{1}{4}$ level teaspoon salt
pepper
1 tablespoon wine vinegar
6 tablespoons soured cream
chopped chives or parsley

Melt the butter in a large saucepan. Add the onion and fry gently until soft but not coloured. Add chopped beetroot and stock and bring slowly to the boil. Cover and simmer gently for 30 minutes. Cool slightly then reduce to a purée by sieving or put in an electric blender in small amounts until a purée. Return to the pan and add salt, pepper and vinegar. Bring back to the boil and simmer gently for 2 to 3 minutes. Serve the soup with a tablespoon of soured cream swirled into each portion and sprinkle with chives or parsley.

Cook's Tip This soup can also be served chilled. In this case, after reducing to a purée add salt, pepper and vinegar and then chill very thoroughly. Serve in bowls again garnished with soured cream and chives or parsley as above.

Easy Tomato Soup
(for four to six)

2 oz butter
1 large onion, finely chopped
2 oz flour
1 pint water
1 pint milk
5 oz can tomato purée
2 teaspoons caster sugar
salt and pepper
½ teaspoon dried dill
chopped parsley

Melt butter in a saucepan. Add onion and fry, stirring occasionally for 5 minutes or until it is soft but not brown. Stir in flour and continue cooking, stirring constantly, for 1 to 2 minutes. Do not let the flour mixture brown.

Remove the pan from the heat and gradually add water, bring to the boil, then blend in milk, stirring constantly. Stir in the tomato purée, sugar, seasoning and dill.

Return pan to the heat and simmer gently for 15

minutes or until onion is cooked. Taste and add more seasoning if necessary. Sprinkle with parsley.

Cook's Tip Canned tomato purée is an economical way of buying tomato as it is concentrated. When using purée in quantity always add a little sweetening in the form of sugar, redcurrant jelly or other jelly. This will counteract the acidity and make it taste delicious.

Minestrone Chicken Soup
(for six)

1 chicken carcass left from the roast
few parsley stalks
1 oz butter
1 large onion, finely chopped
1 clove garlic, crushed
3 carrots, finely diced
2 sticks celery, finely chopped
1 leek, thinly sliced (optional)
4 tomatoes, peeled and chopped
2 level teaspoons tomato purée
1 level teaspoon salt
pepper to taste
1 bayleaf
3 oz spaghetti, broken into $1\frac{1}{2}$ inch lengths
$\frac{1}{4}$ small cabbage, finely shredded
grated Parmesan cheese

Place broken up chicken carcass in a saucepan with 3 to 4 pints of water and the parsley stalks. Bring to the boil, remove scum, cover and simmer gently for 2 hours. Strain stock. Remove any meat from the carcass and chop finely. Melt butter in a saucepan and fry onion and garlic until they begin to colour. Add carrots, celery and leek (if used) and fry gently for 8 to 10 minutes, stirring frequently. Add $2\frac{1}{2}$ pints chicken stock, tomatoes, tomato purée, salt, pepper and bayleaf and bring to the boil. Cover and simmer gently for about an hour until all vegetables are tender. Add any chicken meat and the spaghetti and continue cooking for 10 minutes, stirring occasionally. Add cabbage and continue for a further 15 minutes. Check seasonings, remove bayleaf and serve sprinkled with Parmesan cheese.

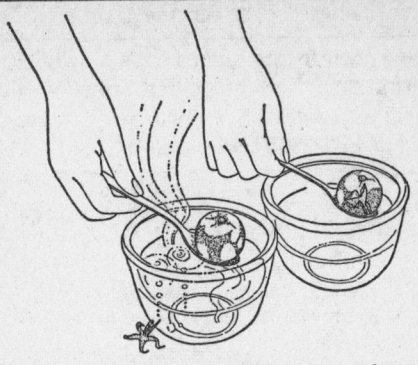

Cook's Tip A quick way to peel tomatoes is to dip them into a basin of boiling water for 8 to 10 seconds, then plunge immediately into cold water. The skins will start to split and then can be easily removed.

Rich Onion Soup
(for four)

2 oz good dripping
1 lb onions, finely chopped
1 oz flour
1½ pints home-made stock *or*
2 chicken stock cubes dissolved in
1½ pints water
salt and pepper
gravy browning
2 oz grated Cheddar cheese

In a large saucepan melt dripping. Add onions and fry them gently, stirring occasionally, until they are beginning to brown. Stir in flour and cook, stirring constantly, until flour mixture is browned.

Gradually add stock, stirring constantly. Add seasoning, and a little gravy browning to give a good colour. Bring to the boil and simmer, covered, for 40 minutes.

Sprinkle with cheese when serving.

Cook's Tip When frying onions cook slowly, turning frequently so that they become golden brown without catching at the edges. A dark brown or black colour means that the soup will be bitter, so take care.

Scottish Vegetable Soup
(for four to six)

1 smoked knuckle of bacon, soaked overnight
1 oz dripping
1 large onion, chopped
3 carrots, diced
2 potatoes, diced
3 celery stalks, sliced
1 bayleaf
salt and pepper
4 oz packet frozen peas

Place bacon knuckle in a saucepan and cover it with cold water. Bring to the boil and drain off water. Add 2 pints of fresh cold water and bring to the boil. Cover pan and simmer for 40 minutes.

Melt dripping in a large saucepan. Add vegetables and fry, stirring occasionally, for 5 minutes. Drain cooking liquid from the bacon knuckle and add it to the vegetables with bayleaf and seasoning. Cover and simmer for 30 minutes.

Meanwhile remove skin and fat from the bacon knuckle. Cut meat into small pieces. Add meat to the soup with peas and cook for a further 5 minutes.

Taste the soup and add more seasoning if necessary. Remove bayleaf and serve with bread rolls and cheese.

Cook's Tip Main meal soups like this one can be made with meaty bones. Apart from bacon knuckle, the best ones being beef and chicken. Go easy on the salt if using bacon: make sure to taste first.

Spinach Soup
(for four)

½ lb spinach or spinach beet
2 oz butter
1 small onion, chopped
1½ pints home-made stock *or*
2 chicken stock cubes dissolved in
1½ pints water
about ¼ level teaspoon salt
pepper
1 tablespoon lemon juice
1 bayleaf
large pinch of ground nutmeg
¼ pint single cream
fried bread croûtons

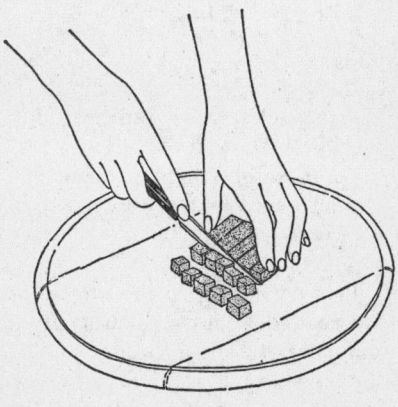

Wash the spinach thoroughly and discard the stalks. Roughly chop the spinach. Melt butter in a saucepan and fry onion gently until soft. Add spinach and toss gently for 5 minutes, stirring frequently without browning. Add stock, salt, pepper, lemon juice, bayleaf and nutmeg and bring to the boil. Cover pan and simmer gently for 25 to 30 minutes. Remove bayleaf and cool soup slightly. Reduce to a purée by sieving or put in an electric blender in small amounts until a purée. Return to the pan, check seasonings and bring back to the boil for 2 minutes. Just before serving, stir in the cream. This soup can also be served chilled in which case, after reducing to a purée and checking seasonings, cool then chill thoroughly. Before serving stir in the cream.

Cook's Tip To make croûtons, cut 2 slices of bread $\frac{1}{2}$ inch thick and remove crusts. Dice the bread. Melt 2 oz butter in a small frying pan and fry the bread cubes slowly until golden brown all over. Drain on absorbent paper and serve hot in a small bowl.

If you prefer thickish soup, add a level tablespoon of flour blended with 3 tablespoons of cold stock or water. Add this after stirring in the $1\frac{1}{2}$ pints of stock.

Kipper Pâté
(for four)

10 oz packet frozen buttered kipper
    fillets, thawed
$\frac{1}{4}$ pint double cream
pinch of cayenne pepper
sprig parsley

Cook kipper fillets according to the directions on packet. When they are cooked, remove them from bag. Pour the butter into a mixing bowl and set aside.

Remove all dark skin and any bones from kipper fillets.

Add kipper fillets to bowl with cream and cayenne. Mash ingredients together with a fork until mixture is smooth. Alternatively, mix all the ingredients together in an electric blender.

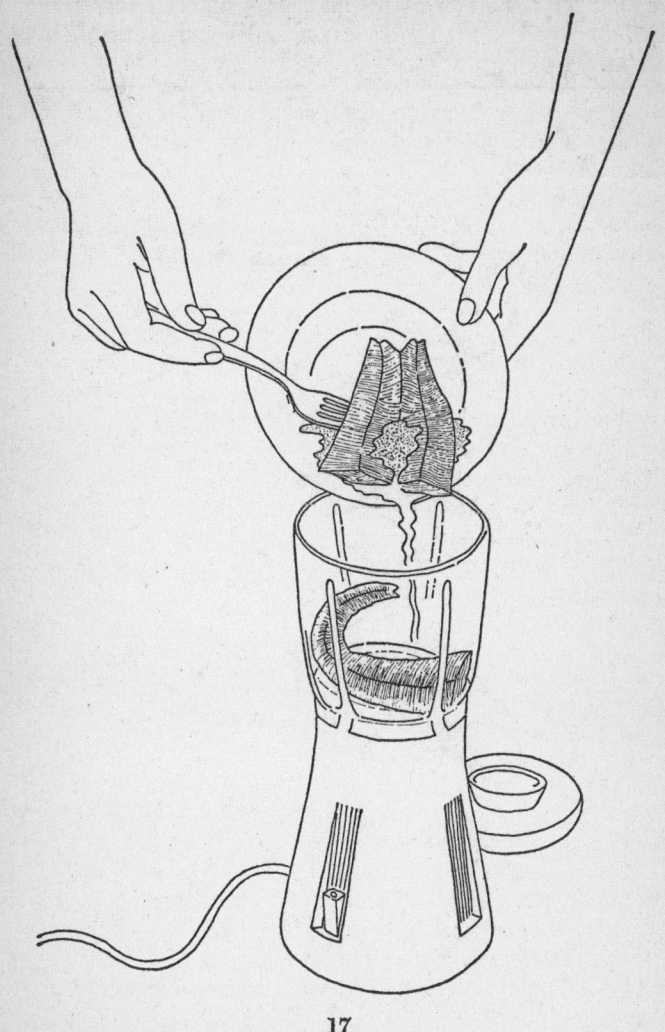

Spoon pâté into a serving dish and smooth the top. Chill for at least 2 hours. Garnish with parsley and serve with hot toast and butter.

Cook's Tip Left overs of this pâté – unlikely that there will be any as it is so good – make a delicious brown bread sandwich filling.

family main dishes

BEEF

Meat per head

Allow 1 lb–1½ lb meat for four people. If only 1 lb meat used, it is best to put plenty of vegetables in the casserole or serve with extra vegetables.

Bristol Beef Casserole
(for four)

1 lb stewing steak
3 carrots, peeled
3 onions, peeled
1 small can tomato soup
(the small can when emptied,
filled with cold water)
1 oz flour
1 stock cube
salt and pepper
pinch mixed herbs

Cut steak into 1 inch pieces. Chop carrots and onions roughly. Put meat and vegetables with the tomato soup into an overproof casserole. Add flour blended with cold water, stock cube and plenty of seasoning and the herbs. Stir until smooth. Cook at 325 deg. F., or gas no. 3 for about 3½ hours according to the cut of stewing steak used.

Cook's Tip The great joy of this casserole is that it can be in the oven in 10 minutes and then it just cooks itself. You would never guess the basis was a can of tomato soup.

Family Meat Loaf
(for four)

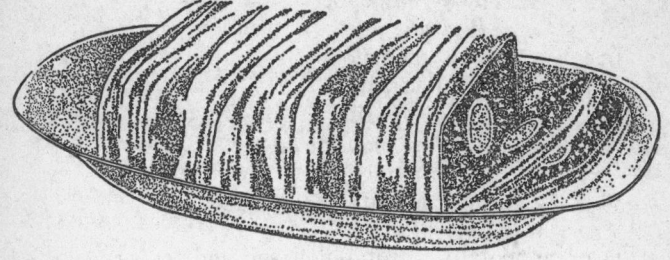

6 rashers streaky bacon
1 lb best quality minced beef
1 clove garlic, crushed
1 oz white breadcrumbs
12 pimento stuffed olives, halved
1 level teaspoon salt
ground black pepper
1 egg to mix
3 hard-boiled eggs, shelled

Line a greased 1 lb loaf tin with streaky bacon. Mix mince, garlic, olives, breadcrumbs and seasonings. Blend with egg. Put half mixture in loaf tin. Arrange eggs in line over mince mixture, top with remainder of mince. Cover with greased foil. Bake at 350 deg. F., or gas no. 4, for 1 hour. Leave in tin to become cold, then turn out and serve in slices.

Cook's Tip Serve this loaf in summer with French bread, salads and chutney. Chill before slicing otherwise it is inclined to crumble.

Slade's Pie
(for six)

1 lb raw minced beef
6 oz potatoes, finely diced
4 oz carrots, finely diced (optional)
1 large onion, finely chopped
1½ level teaspoons salt
plenty of pepper
Pastry:
12 oz plain flour
pinch of salt
3 oz margarine
3 oz lard or white fat
water to mix
milk or beaten egg to glaze

Place beef, potato, carrot, onion, salt and pepper in a bowl and mix thoroughly. Sieve the flour and salt into a bowl and rub in the fats until mixture resembles fine breadcrumbs. Add sufficient water to mix to a pliable dough. On a floured surface roll out ⅔ pastry to an oblong and use to line a deep swiss roll tin (approx 11″ × 7″ × 1½″). Lay meat mixture in pastry and press down evenly. Roll remaining pastry into an oblong for the lid. Damp edges of pie, position lid and press edges well together. Trim off surplus and crimp the edge. Decorate top with pastry trimmings. Brush with milk or egg and bake in preheated oven at 425 deg. F., or gas no. 7, for 20 to 25 minutes until lightly browned, then reduce temperature to 350 deg. F., or gas no. 4, and continue for 35 to 40 minutes. Serve hot.

Cook's Tip This mixture can be used to make traditional Cornish pasties by cutting out a piece of pastry the size of a saucer, placing meat in the middle and pulling the edges up together at the top. Press well together and crimp. Cook as for the pie but allow 5 to 10 minutes less. The mixture can also be used to fill puff pastry pasties.

Summer Casserole
(for four to six)

1½ oz dripping
1½ lbs stewing steak cut in 1 inch cubes
1½ oz flour
1 large onion, sliced
¼ pint home-made stock *or*
1 beef stock cube dissolved in
¼ pint water
1 tablespoon Worcester sauce
2 tablespoons Soy sauce
1 rounded tablespoon redcurrant jelly
1 lb ripe tomatoes
salt and pepper

Heat dripping in a frying pan, toss meat in flour and fry for 5 minutes or until browned, remove from pan and place in a 3½ pint casserole. Add onion to fat remaining in pan and fry for 2 to 3 minutes, add to the meat. Stir remaining flour into fat in pan and cook for 1 minute. Add stock and stir until blended, stir in Worcester sauce, Soy sauce and redcurrant jelly and pour over the meat and onions. Peel and roughly chop tomatoes and add to casserole with salt and pepper. Cover casserole and cook in the oven preheated to 325 deg. F., or gas no. 3, for 2 to 3 hours until tender.

Cook's Tip If tomatoes are not reasonable in price at the time that you are making this casserole, add instead a 14 oz can of tomatoes, with the juices from the can.

Slow Roasted Brisket
(for six to eight)

3½ lb lean brisket, boned and rolled
½–¾ pint home-made stock *or*
1 beef stock cube dissolved in
½–¾ pint water

Ask your butcher to prepare the brisket for you by removing all the excess fat and the bone. Put meat in a small meat tin, pour in 1 inch of stock. Season meat with salt or pepper. Cover tin with foil. Put in the oven preheated to 425 deg. F., or gas no. 7, for 30 minutes, lower oven to 300 deg. F., or gas no. 2, for 40 minutes per lb of meat. Turn oven up to 400 deg. F., or gas no. 6, for the last half hour for the Yorkshire puddings and to finish browning the potatoes. Make the gravy with the stock and juices of the meat.

Cook's Tip A good lean piece of brisket slow roasts beautifully. Don't expect the middle to be pink, but do expect it to be tender. It makes an economical Sunday roast.

Beef Goulash
(for four to six)

1 oz lard
1 lb onions, sliced
1½ lb chuck steak, cut into 1 inch cubes
1 tablespoon paprika (or more, if liked)
1 pint home-made stock *or*
2 beef stock cubes dissolved in
1 pint water
salt and pepper
2 tablespoons flour
2 tablespoons tomato purée
5 oz soured cream

In a frying pan or 3 pint flameproof casserole, melt lard. Add onions and fry, stirring occasionally, until they are lightly browned. If using a frying pan, transfer onions to a casserole.

Quickly brown beef in melted lard and transfer to casserole. Add paprika, stock and seasoning to the casserole and stir well. Cover casserole and put in the oven preheated to 350 deg. F., or gas no. 4. Cook for 1½ hours.

Mix together flour and tomato purée. Remove casserole from the oven and stir in flour mixture. Place casserole over a moderate heat and bring to the boil stirring. Simmer until liquid has thickened. Taste and add more salt and pepper if necessary.

Spoon over the soured cream.

Cook's Tip To make this really traditional, add cubes of raw potato half way through the cooking time.

Carbonnade of Beef

(for four to six)

1½ lbs chuck steak, cut into ½ inch thick strips
1 oz butter
2 tablespoons oil
2 medium sized onions chopped
2 tablespoons flour
½ pint light ale
¼ pint water
pinch of dried thyme
1 bayleaf
1 teaspoon sugar
1 teaspoon salt
freshly ground black pepper

Brown meat quickly in butter and oil in a saucepan. Remove meat strips from pan and set aside. Add onions to the pan and fry until they are golden brown. Blend in flour and cook for 1 minute. Remove pan from the heat and gradually add light ale and water, stirring constantly.

Return to the heat and bring to the boil. Simmer until mixture has thickened. Add meat strips to the pan with thyme, bayleaf, sugar, salt and pepper. Cover and simmer for 2 hours or until the meat is tender. Remove bayleaf.

Cook's Tip Once beer or cider is opened and used for cooking, any that is left should be decanted into a small bottle and kept in the refrigerator. Use within 2 weeks.

Beef Stew with Herb Dumplings
(for four)

1 lb shin of beef
1 oz flour
2 carrots
1 parsnip
2 onions
3 outside sticks of celery
1 oz dripping
¾ pint home-made stock *or*
1 beef stock cube dissolved in
¾ pint water
salt and pepper
bayleaf
Herb Dumplings:
4 oz self-raising flour
2 oz prepared shredded suet
½ level teaspoon salt
1 level tablespoon freshly chopped herbs
about 5 to 6 tablespoons water

Trim the excess fat from the meat and cut into 1 inch cubes, toss in flour.

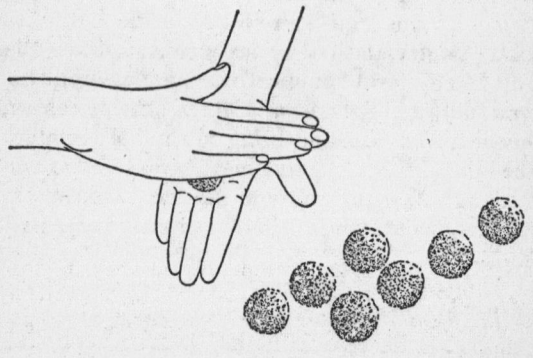

Peel and slice carrots, peel parsnip and cut into $\frac{1}{2}$ inch dice. Peel and quarter the onions, wash and slice the celery. Melt the dripping in a pan and fry the meat for 3 to 4 minutes. Stir in any remaining flour. Add vegetables, water, stock cube, seasoning and bayleaf, bring to the boil, stirring. Cover and simmer for $2\frac{1}{2}$ to $3\frac{1}{2}$ hours or until tender. Remove bayleaf.

Prepare the dumplings. Sift the flour into a bowl and stir in the suet, salt and herbs. Mix to a soft but not sticky dough with the water. Form into 8 small balls.

Place on top of the stew, cover and cook very gently, simmering for a further 30 minutes until well risen.

Turn into a serving dish and serve at once.

Cook's Tip If you can get it, use butcher's beef suet, it is cheaper but you do have to grate it coarsely yourself.

Pressed Beef
(for six)

$2\frac{1}{2}$–3 lb salted brisket of beef, boned
1 large onion, roughly chopped
8 cloves
3 bayleaves
2 carrots, sliced
2 sticks celery, sliced (optional)
8 peppercorns

Place the brisket in a saucepan just large enough to take it. Add sufficient water just to cover the joint. Surround with all the other ingredients. Bring to the boil slowly then scoop off any scum. Cover pan and simmer very gently for 3 to $3\frac{1}{2}$ hours until very tender. It may be necessary to add a little more boiling water during the cooking time. Remove meat carefully and pick off any cloves or peppercorns which may still be attached. Place carefully in a cake tin which is just a little too small for the meat. Cover with a saucer or plate and then several weights. Leave until cold and then chill for several hours. To serve turn the meat out carefully and cut downwards into thin slices. Serve with salads.

Cook's Tip If possible, give your butcher a week's warning so that he can salt the beef specially for you. The time taken in the brine varies according to the strength of the brine. With larger pieces of brisket the pressing and weighting of the cooked meat used to be done between two wooden boards. If there is not a suitable size container available for the meat, two clean chopping boards or plates and a few heavy tins will do the trick.

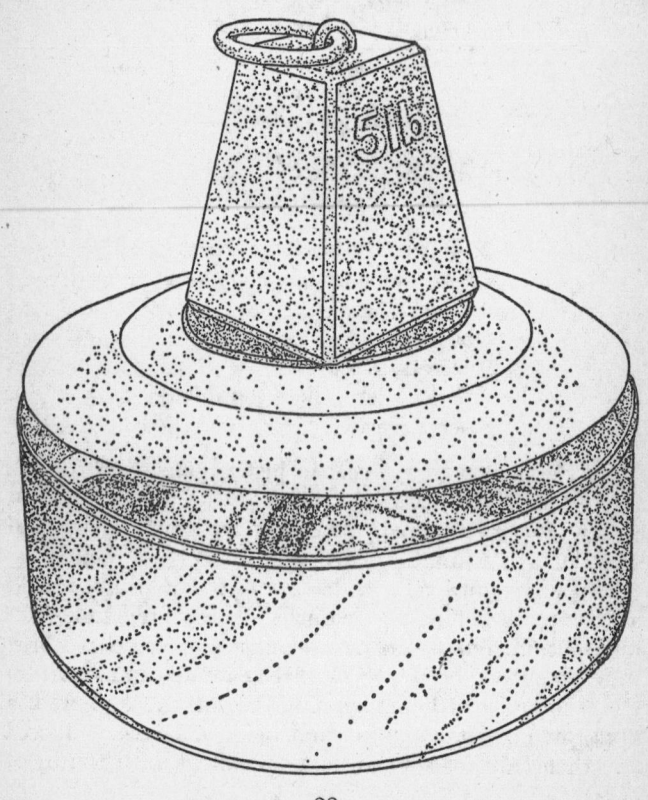

Pot Roast Brisket

(for six)

2½ lb boned and rolled brisket of fresh beef
little dripping or oil
4 carrots, thickly sliced
4 onions, each cut into eight
6 sticks celery, cut into 1 inch lengths
10 cloves
10 peppercorns
2 bayleaves
1 stock cube
½ pint hot water
1 level teaspoon salt
pepper
1 level tablespoon cornflour

Brown the joint all over in the hot dripping in a frying pan, then place it in a deep casserole or small roasting tin, or brown in a very hot oven in the meat tin if the oven is being used. Lay carrots, onions and celery about the joint then sprinkle the cloves and peppercorns all around. Add bayleaves. Dissolve stock cube in the hot water and add salt and pepper. Pour around the joint and cover the casserole with a lid or the roasting tin with foil. Cook at 325 deg. F., or gas no. 3, for 3 to 3½ hours or until tender. Remove meat to a hot serving dish; drain vegetables and place in a dish then strain cooking liquor into a saucepan. Spoon off any excess fat, then thicken with the cornflour blended in a little cold water. Bring to the boil for 3 minutes, check seasonings and serve with the joint.

Cook's Tip This dish can be served cold equally well. Cool completely in the casserole then remove and chill. Serve cut in thin slices. Remove cloves, peppercorns, and bayleaves from vegetables then reduce to a purée by sieving or put in the blender in small amounts until a purée to make soup. Add sufficient beef stock and seasonings to give the desired consistency and flavour.

Ways of Using Raw Minced Beef

(All recipes are for four)

BASIC SAVOURY MINCE

small knob dripping *or*
few bacon rinds
1 lb fresh minced beef
1 large onion, chopped
¼ teaspoon mixed dried herbs
1 oz flour
½ pint water
salt and freshly-ground pepper
little gravy browning

Melt dripping in pan or extract fat from bacon rinds then throw them away. Add meat and brown – stirring frequently. Stir in onion, herbs and flour – cook for about 1 minute. Blend in water, season, add gravy browning if liked. Bring to the boil and simmer for at least one hour, preferably longer.

Cook's Tip When choosing mince, the colour should be red, not white or brown. Cook the day you buy. The quality of the mince is very important. Cuts of meat used in everyday mince are leg of beef, shin, flank and possibly brisket. Best mince requires a shorter cooking time. Cuts are usually chuck and bladebone, and sometimes end silverside.

COTTAGE PIE
(Using basic savoury mince ingredients)

Put in 2 pint dish. Top with 1 lb cooked mashed potatoes, seasoned well. Add for a change grated cheese or juice of garlic. Dot with butter. Bake in preheated oven at 425 deg. F., or gas no. 7, for about 20 minutes or until brown.

STUFFED CABBAGE LEAVES

Make a basic savoury mince mixture with only ¼ pint water. Take 8 cabbage leaves, remove their centre stalks and place them in boiling water for 3 minutes to soften and blanch them. Divide mixture amongst the 8 leaves and roll up. Turn a 16 oz can of tomatoes into an oven-proof casserole; add 2 sliced onions and 2 sliced potatoes, a little Worcester sauce, sugar and seasoning. Arrange cabbage leaf parcels on top. Cover and bake for 50 minutes in oven preheated to 350 deg. F., or gas no. 4, until vegetables are tender.

BOLOGNAISE OR TOMATO MINCE

Add 4 sticks chopped celery to basic mince before cooking. Add 2 tablespoons tomato purée, 2 tablespoons ketchup, a little sugar and garlic powder.

CHILLI CON CARNE

Cook peppers with basic mince. Add 16 oz can of red kidney beans, and 8 oz can tomatoes, 1 teaspoon of chilli powder and 2 tablespoons dried pepper flakes.

HOME-MADE BEEFBURGERS

- 8 oz raw minced beef
- 8 oz pork sausagemeat
- ¼ teaspoon nutmeg
- ½ teaspoon salt
- ⅛ teaspoon ground black pepper
- 1 medium finely chopped onion

Blend all ingredients together. Flour hands, roll mixture into 8 balls, flatten out to 3½ inch beefburgers. Grill or fry in very little dripping for 2½ minutes each side.

Put between baps or top with slice of cheese, dust with paprika pepper and grill to brown, or serve fried egg on top and call it Holstein.

LAMB

Boned Shoulder of Lamb with Savoury Green Stuffing
(for six)

3 lb shoulder of lamb, boned
salt and pepper
Stuffing:
1 oz butter
1 tablespoon oil
1 onion, chopped
4 oz lambs' liver, in small pieces
2 oz fresh white breadcrumbs
½ bunch watercress, finely chopped
1 small clove garlic, crushed
½ level teaspoon chopped rosemary

Open out shoulder and flatten. Season with salt and pepper. Melt butter, add oil. Fry onion until soft, add liver and fry

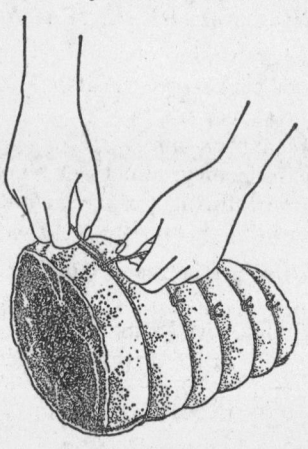

for 1 minute. Add other ingredients, season and use to stuff lamb. Roll up and tie with fine string at 1½ inch intervals. Place in a roasting tin and set this in the preheated oven at 325 deg. F., or gas no. 3, to roast for 40 minutes per lb, plus 40 minutes over. Make gravy from juices in the tin.

Cook's Tip New Zealand lamb is ideal cooked in this way. If watercress is not available use masses of chopped parsley mixed with a little chopped thyme. There will be lots of juices in the meat tin for gravy.

Stuffed Apricot Lamb
(for four to six)

3 breasts of lamb *or* a small boned
    shoulder of lamb
1 onion, chopped
½ oz butter
7¾ oz can apricot halves
2 oz fresh breadcrumbs
2 tablespoons chopped parsley
½ level teaspoon salt
pepper
1 egg, beaten
little dripping

Remove skin and bones from each breast of lamb, then take out any excess fat. Fry onion in the butter in a small pan until golden brown. Drain apricots (reserving juice to use in gravy) and roughly chop. Mix onion with the apricots, breadcrumbs, parsley, salt and pepper and bind together with the beaten egg. Spread stuffing over the inside of two pieces of lamb and cover with the third; or spread over the inside of the shoulder of lamb, carefully roll up tightly and secure with skewers and string. Weigh joint. Stand in a roasting tin and surround with a little roast

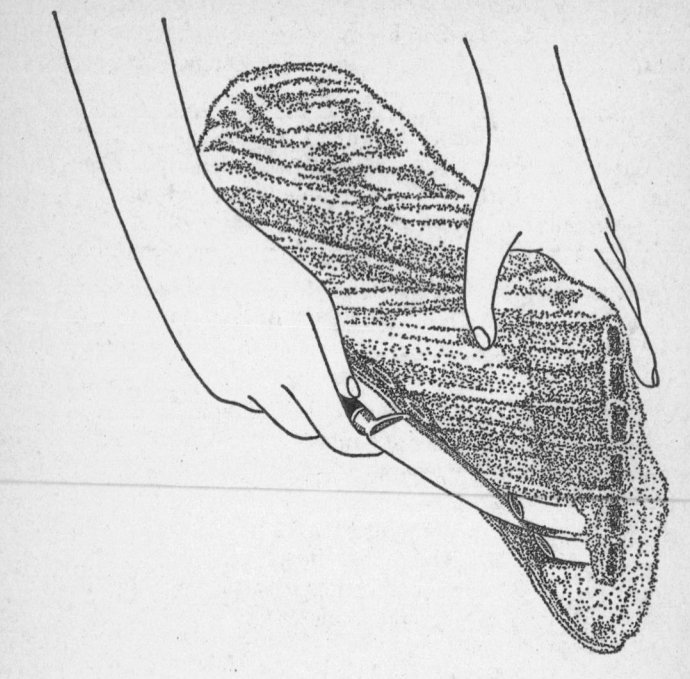

dripping. Sprinkle lightly with salt and cook in preheated oven at 400 deg. F., or gas no. 6, allowing 25 minutes per lb plus 30 minutes over. Baste occasionally and cover top of joint with foil when sufficiently browned. Serve with a gravy made with usual ingredients and the apricot juice.

Cook's Tip Use the bones from the breast of lamb to make a stock for a family soup. When cold, chill thoroughly so that the fat will solidify and can be easily removed before beginning to make the soup.

Irish Stew
(for four to six)

2½ lb middle neck *or* scrag of lamb
1 lb onions, sliced
2 lb potatoes, sliced
salt and pepper
1 teaspoon chopped fresh thyme *or*
    ½ teaspoon dried thyme
water

Remove spinal cord and trim fat from the lamb. Cut meat into convenient sized pieces. Put half the onions into a 3 pint casserole, add half the potatoes and then the meat. Season each layer well. Add thyme and enough water just

to cover, then make a layer of remaining onions and top with potatoes.

Cover casserole and put it in the oven preheated to 325 deg. F., or gas no. 3. Cook for 1 hour. Remove the lid and cook for a further hour. Serve with braised carrots cooked in the oven at the same time as the stew.

Cook's Tip   The bones of Irish stew are often not popular, so you can use lean pieces of lamb fillet from the neck. 1 lb would be the amount needed.

Red Hot Lamb
(for four)

2 breasts of lamb *or* 2 lb middle neck lamb
2 tablespoons dripping *or* oil
2 onions, sliced
1 glove garlic, crushed
1 level tablespoon curry powder
1 level tablespoon flour
2 level teaspoons tomato purée
$\frac{3}{4}$ pint home-made stock *or*
1 beef stock cube dissolved in
$\frac{3}{4}$ pint water
15 oz can peeled tomatoes
4 large carrots, sliced (optional)
$\frac{3}{4}$ level teaspoon salt
pepper

Remove skin and excess fat from the breasts of lamb then cut into even sized pieces. Trim excess fat from the middle neck pieces if used. Fry lamb in the dripping or oil until browned all over. Drain well and transfer to a $4\frac{1}{2}$ to 5 pint casserole. Drain off all fat except 1 tablespoon from the pan, then fry onions and garlic until browned. Stir in curry powder, flour and tomato purée, then gradually add stock and bring to the boil, stirring frequently. Add can of tomatoes including juice, carrots if used, salt and pepper, bring back to the boil and simmer for 2 minutes. Pour over lamb, cover casserole and cook in the oven preheated to 325 deg. F., or gas no. 3, for about 2 hours until tender. Check seasoning. Spoon off excess fat from the casserole before serving.

Cook's Tip If you like it really hot, double the curry powder in the recipe. It is easier to remove all the fat from this casserole if, the day before required, it is cooked for $1\frac{1}{2}$ hours, then cooled and chilled. Before reheating at the same temperature for 1 to $1\frac{1}{4}$ hours, lift off all the solid fat from the surface.

Suety Pudding
(for four)

2 oz lamb dripping from the roasting tin
1½ oz prepared shredded suet
4 oz self-raising flour
½ level teaspoon salt
1 egg
3 tablespoons milk

Heat the oven to 400 deg. F., or gas no. 6. Place the dripping in a round, shallow, 1 pint ovenproof tin or dish and heat until very hot.

Sift the flour into a basin, stir in the suet and salt. Lightly beat the egg and add with the milk to the mixture and mix to a soft but not sticky dough.

Pat out the dough to the size of the dish on a lightly floured table. Put straight into the hot dripping, return to the oven and cook for about 20 minutes, until golden brown. Remove from oven. Cut in wedges. Serve with roast lamb, gravy and vegetables just as you would Yorkshire pudding with beef.

Cook's Tip Make this pudding while roasting the joint and use the dripping from the meat tin. The better the flavour of the dripping, the nicer the pudding.

LIVER

Liver Kebabs

(for four)

2 tablespoons oil
2 tablespoons vinegar
2 tablespoons lemon juice
½ level teaspoon salt
pepper to taste
1 clove garlic, crushed
1 teaspoon Worcester sauce
1 lb lambs' liver in one piece
8 rashers streaky bacon, de-rinded
8 flat mushrooms

Glory Farm Barbecue sauce:

1 oz butter
1 small onion, finely chopped
4 tablespoons tomato ketchup
2 tablespoons vinegar
2 level tablespoons mango chutney, chopped
¼ teaspoon French mustard
1 teaspoon caster sugar
1 tablespoon Worcester sauce

Place oil, vinegar, lemon juice, salt, pepper, garlic and Worcester sauce in a bowl. Cut the liver into 1 inch cubes, Place liver in the marinade and leave for several hours, turning once or twice. Make the bacon into tight rolls. Dip mushrooms in the marinade. On 4 long skewers thread alternately pieces of liver, mushrooms and bacon rolls. Cook under a moderate grill for about 5 minutes each side, brushing kebabs with marinade once or twice during cooking, until liver is just cooked but not overdone.

To make the sauce: melt the butter, fry onion gently until tender without colouring. Add rest of ingredients, bring to the boil. Serve hot or cold with the kebabs.

Cook's Tip The sauce can be served with many other dishes including chops, fried chicken, steaks, etc. Sliced button mushrooms can be added too, at the end.

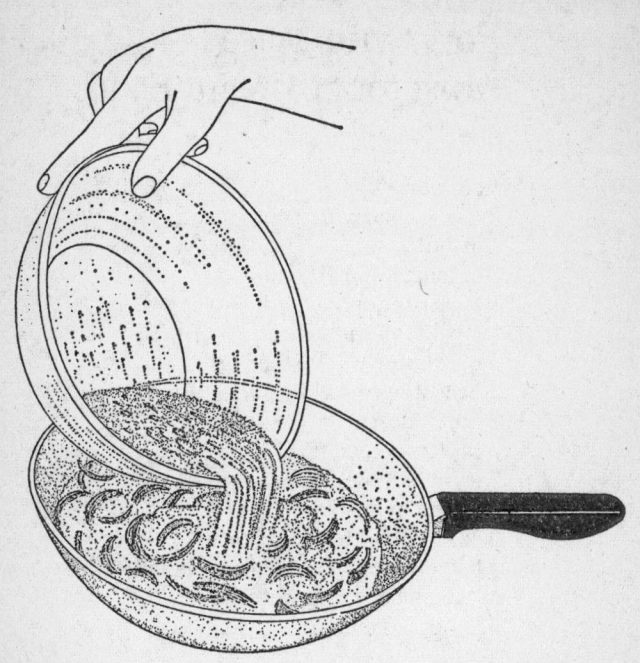

PORK AND BACON

Pork with Spiced Mushroom Cream Sauce
(for four)

1¼ lb pork fillet
2 tablespoons salad oil
1 oz butter
1 onion, chopped
1 level tablespoon paprika pepper
1 level tablespoon flour
1 pint home-made stock *or*
1 beef stock cube dissolved in
1 pint water
5 tablespoons sherry
1 level teaspoon tomato purée
salt and pepper
6 oz small button mushrooms
1 level tablespoon cornflour mixed with
2 tablespoons cold water
5 oz soured cream

Cut pork in 1½ inch pieces. Heat oil in a pan, add butter then fry pork pieces quickly until they are just beginning to brown. Remove from pan and drain on kitchen paper. Add onion and paprika to pan and fry for 2 minutes. Blend in flour and cook for a further minute. Remove from heat and stir in stock, sherry and tomato purée, return to the heat and simmer until thick. Season with salt and pepper, then return meat to pan, cover and simmer for 30 to 40 minutes or until pork is tender. Wash mushrooms and add to pan. Add mixed cornflour to pan. Bring to boil, stirring. Just before serving, blend in the soured cream and check seasoning. Turn pork mixture onto a serving dish and, if liked, garnish with triangles of fried bread and sprigs of parsley.

Cook's Tip Take care not to boil the sauce, having added the soured cream, if you do, it will curdle. To sour fresh double cream if soured cream is not available just stir in 2 tablespoons fresh lemon juice.

Pork Chops with Cider and Mushroom Sauce
(for six)

6 pork chops
salt and pepper
8 oz button mushrooms
2 oz butter
1½ oz flour
½ pint cider
pinch of dried mixed herbs
¼ pint single cream

Remove the rack from grill pan and line pan with a piece of foil. Lay chops on this and season well with salt and pepper. Grill chops for about 15 minutes, turning once, or until they are crisp and brown. Transfer the chops to a serving dish and keep hot. Reserve the juices on the foil.

Fry the mushrooms gently in the butter for 2 minutes. Remove them from the pan. Stir the flour into the butter and cook, stirring, for 1 minute. Gradually add the cider, stirring constantly. Blend in reserved meat juices and herbs and bring to the boil, stirring. Return mushrooms to the sauce and simmer for 3 to 4 minutes, stirring constantly or until the sauce has thickened.

Add cream and heat gently. Do not allow to boil. Serve with sauce poured over chops.

Cook's Tip If the sauce for the chops has to be kept hot, omit the cream and add at the very last moment, otherwise the whole lot may well curdle.

Pork Chops in Barbecue Sauce
(for four)

4 pork chops

Sauce:

8 tablespoons tomato ketchup
2 tablespoons Soy sauce
2 tablespoons malt vinegar
1 tablespoon Worcester sauce
2 teaspoons caster sugar
2 garlic cloves, crushed
salt and pepper

Turn on the grill to hot. Line grill pan with aluminium foil leaving plenty hanging over sides. Remove rind and fat from pork chops and arrange them on foil. Place them under grill and cook for 2 minutes on each side, or until chops are well browned.

Meanwhile mix all the sauce ingredients together and set aside. Pour off excess fat from grill pan. Lift foil case containing chops and place it on a flat ovenproof dish or baking sheet. Pour over sauce and cover chops with another piece of foil. Fold the edges of foil together to seal.

Place dish or baking sheet in the oven preheated to 350 deg. F., or gas no. 4, and cook for 1 hour.

Cook's Tip Garlic for most recipes is far better crushed in a garlic press. You then only get the juice and none of the fibre or pieces.

Spicy Pork Balls
(for four)

2 pork knuckles or hocks
2 onions, peeled
2 oz fresh breadcrumbs
½ level teaspoon salt
pepper to taste
1 egg, beaten
little flour
2 tablespoons oil
4 level tablespoons brown sugar
1 level teaspoon paprika
1 level tablespoon tomato purée
1 level teaspoon salt
1 tablespoon Worcester sauce
bare ½ pint water
3 tablespoons lemon juice
2 tablespoons malt vinegar
8 prunes, soaked

Remove skin from the pork knuckles then strip flesh from the bones. Discard any excess fat and gristle. Put through a fine mincer together with 1 onion. Combine minced pork, onion, breadcrumbs, salt and pepper and bind together with the egg. Divide into 12 and shape into even sized balls. Lightly coat in flour. Heat oil in a pan and fry meatballs until browned all over. Drain well and place in a 3 pint casserole.

Slice remaining onion and fry in the same oil until golden brown then drain off all the fat. Mix together all the other ingredients except prunes and add to the onions in the pan. Bring to the boil, simmer for 1 minute then pour over meatballs. Cover casserole and cook in preheated oven at 325 deg. F., or gas no. 3, for 45 minutes. Add prunes and continue cooking for about 15 minutes. Spoon off any excess fat and serve.

Cook's Tip These pork knuckles or hocks also make excellent cheap and tasty roasts. Score skin then rub with salt and place in a baking tin with a little dripping and a few peeled potatoes. Cook at 425 deg. F., or gas no. 7, for 1 to 1¼ hours until tender, basting once or twice.

Crunchy Pork and Cabbage
(for four)

1¼–1½ lb lean belly of pork
2 oz butter
2 large onions, sliced
2 cloves garlic, crushed
8 oz carrots, diced
2 level teaspoons curry powder
1 tablespoon Soy sauce
¾ level teaspoon salt
pepper to taste
3 tablespoons water
8 oz white cabbage, *or*
    heart of a cabbage, shredded
8 oz frozen peas

Remove skin from the pork and then cut away any bones and hard gristle. Cut pork into neat cubes. Heat butter in a pan and add the pork. Fry gently for 5 minutes, stirring frequently. Add onions, garlic, and carrots and continue gently for 10 to 15 minutes, stirring occasionally to prevent sticking. Stir in the curry powder, Soy sauce, salt, pepper and water and cover pan. Simmer gently for 15 to 20 minutes until the pork is tender, stirring occasionally. Meanwhile cook cabbage and peas for 3 to 5 minutes in boiling salted water until cabbage is still very crisp but just tender; drain. Add the cabbage and peas. Blend well, check seasoning and serve at once.

Cook's Tip This dish can be prepared in advance as far as simmering until tender with all ingredients added except peas and cabbage; then cool quickly. Just before serving, cook cabbage and peas and continue as above.

Apple Baked Collar
(for eight)

3 lb collar of bacon
¾ pint apple juice
1 onion, thinly sliced
freshly ground black pepper
2 tablespoons honey
3 Cox's apples, sliced and cored
2 oz demerara sugar
1 oz butter
2 tablespoons oil
1 tablespoon cornflour mixed with
1 tablespoon water (optional)

Soak collar in cold water for 12 hours or overnight. Drain and place it in a saucepan. Pour over apple juice, adding more if necessary so that the joint is just covered. Add onions and pepper, cover and bring to the boil. Simmer for 1¼ hours or 20 minutes to the pound plus 20 minutes over. Take collar out of pan and cool slightly.

Remove the skin from collar and score fat diagonally across in diamond shapes. Place in a shallow ovenproof dish. Brush with honey. Bake in the centre of a very hot

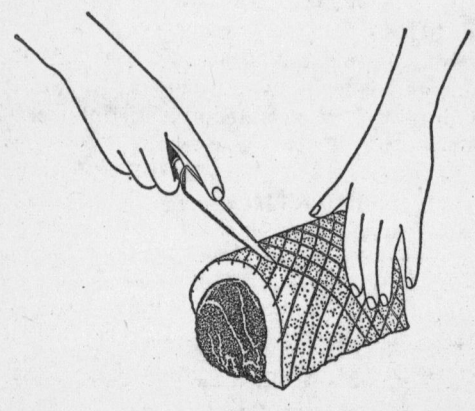

oven 425 deg. F., or gas no. 7, for 15 minutes or until the joint is golden.

Meanwhile toss apple rings in sugar. Fry them in butter and oil until they are golden brown and the sugar and fat have formed a syrup.

Place collar on a serving dish and garnish with apple rings. If you like, thicken apple juice with blended cornflour, re-heat and serve with the collar as a sauce.

Cook's Tip To prevent bacon joints shrinking whilst they are being simmered, it is essential that the water bubbles very gently and doesn't actually boil during the cooking time.

Golden Nuggets
(for four)

8 oz long grain rice
salt and pepper
1 egg, beaten
4 oz lean cooked ham
4 oz Cheddar cheese, finely grated
good pinch of powdered garlic
3–4 tablespoons chutney sauce *or* brown table sauce
golden breadcrumbs *or* browned breadcrumbs
dripping *or* oil for frying

Cook rice in plenty of boiling salted water until just tender – 12 to 14 minutes – then drain, rinse under hot running water and then drain again very thoroughly. Season the beaten egg with ½ level teaspoon salt and pepper to taste then add the hot rice and mix thoroughly. Leave until cool.

Put the meat through the fine blade of a mincer then mix with the cheese, garlic and chutney sauce. Divide into 8 and shape each into a barrel. Divide rice also into 8 and mould around the meat barrels, to completely enclose the filling. Dip each in breadcrumbs. Heat about ½ inch dripping or oil in a frying pan and fry the nuggets for about 10 to 15 minutes until golden brown all over, turning them several times. Drain thoroughly on absorbent paper and serve hot.

Cook's Tip The quickest, easiest and most economical way of coating food in breadcrumbs is to put a small amount in a small polythene bag, add the food to be coated and shake carefully until sufficiently covered. The remaining crumbs can then be used next time.

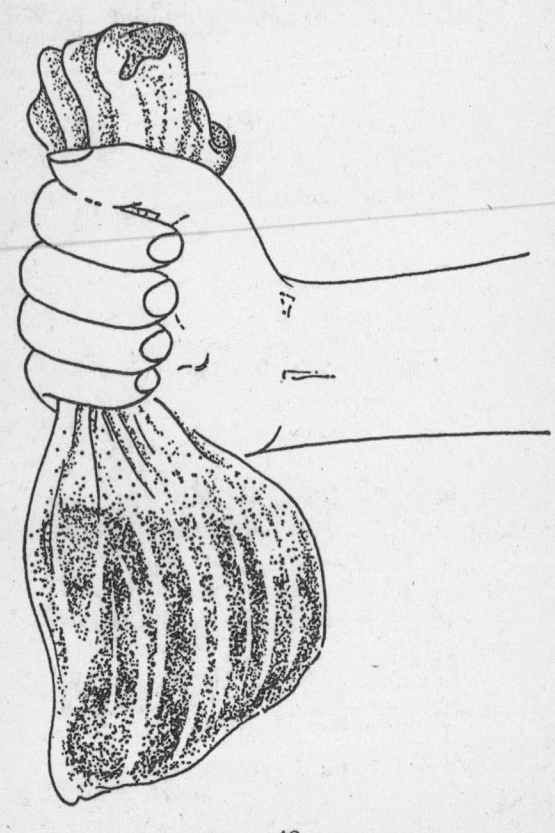

SAUSAGEMEAT

Sausage-Burger Toad in the Hole
(for four to five)

8 oz beef sausagemeat
8 oz raw minced beef
salt and pepper
¼ teaspoon dried mixed herbs
½ oz beef dripping
Batter:
4 oz flour
1 teaspoon salt
1 egg, lightly beaten
½ pint mixed milk and water

Mix sausagemeat, minced beef, seasoning and herbs together thoroughly with your hands. Divide mixture into 6 portions and shape them into patties. Coat them lightly with flour.

Melt the dripping in a 7" × 11" roasting tin. Place the sausage-burger patties in tin and set aside.

To make batter: sift flour and salt into a mixing bowl. Stir in the egg and gradually add the milk and water; mix to a smooth batter.

Pour batter over sausage-burgers and place tin in the oven preheated to 425 deg. F., or gas no. 7. Cook for 35 to 40 minutes or until the batter topping is well risen, crisp and golden brown.

Cook's Tip Use this same recipe for your beefburgers if liked, add fresh herbs in season.

Hunter's Roll

(for six)

Pastry:

8 oz plain flour
pinch of salt
2 oz margarine
2 oz lard *or* white fat
water to mix

Filling:

1 lb pork sausagemeat
6 oz streaky bacon rashers, de-rinded and chopped
1 small onion, finely chopped
1 level teaspoon mixed herbs
½ level teaspoon salt
pepper to taste
3 hard-boiled eggs
beaten egg *or* milk to glaze

Sieve flour and salt together into a bowl and rub in the fats until mixture resembles fine breadcrumbs. Add sufficient water to mix to a pliable dough. Combine sausagemeat, bacon, onion, herbs and salt and pepper. On a lightly floured surface roll out pastry to an oblong, approx 12" × 10", then lay half sausagemeat mixture down the centre.

Place eggs on top in a line then cover with the rest of the sausagemeat. Shape into a neat oblong. Pull edges of pastry over to enclose filling, damp one edge and press well together. Trim ends and press well together. Turn roll over and place on a dampened baking sheet. Decorate with small circles of pastry cut from the trimmings and brush with egg or milk. Make three small slits in the top and cook in preheated oven at 425 deg. F., or gas no. 7, for 20 minutes then reduce to 350 deg. F., or gas no. 4, for a further 30 to 40 minutes until golden brown. Serve hot or cold.

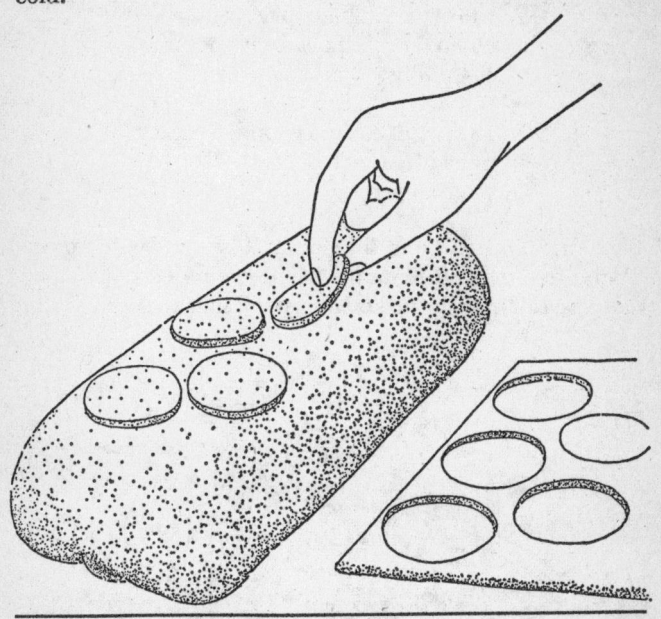

Cook's Tip During cooking some of the juices from sausagemeat will seep out. They should be carefully poured off to prevent making the bottom of the pastry too soggy and to stop excess sticking to the tin. Before removing loosen the roll completely with a palette knife to prevent breaking the pastry.

TURKEY

Spring Turkey Mayonnaise
(for six)

1 small onion, chopped
½ clove garlic
1 tablespoon tomato purée
½ level teaspoon curry powder
1 tablespoon lime juice
about 2 tablespoons apricot jam
¼–½ pint good mayonnaise
salt and pepper
12 oz–1 lb cooked chopped turkey
parsley sprigs
paprika pepper

Put onion and garlic in an electric blender, switch on for 1 minute. Heat all remaining ingredients except mayonnaise, seasoning and turkey in a small pan and bring to the

boil slowly, stirring all the time. Add to blender, switch on and reduce to a purée. Blend with mayonnaise in bowl, add turkey. Season well. Chill overnight in refrigerator before serving. Check seasoning, garnish with parsley and dust with paprika pepper.

To make without a blender: finely chop onion and crush garlic. Put in a pan with all other ingredients except mayonnaise, seasoning and turkey. Bring to the boil slowly, stirring all the time. Sieve mixture and blend with mayonnaise and turkey. Season, chill overnight before serving. Check seasoning, add garnish.

Cook's Tip Make this very mild curried turkey for a party. It can be made the day before and seems very popular. It goes well with most salads and hot new potatoes if in season. A good way of using up turkey legs after the roast.

Toast Hawaii
(for one)

1 thick slice of bread
little butter
little made mustard
1 slice ham
1 slice canned pineapple, drained
1 slice of Cheddar cheese the size of bread
paprika pepper

Toast bread under the grill, remove crusts. Butter toast, then cover with ham, spread with a little mustard, then top with pineapple and lastly cheese. Sprinkle with a dusting of paprika pepper. Slip under a hot grill to brown. Serve at once.

Cook's Tip Sprinkling the cheese with mild paprika pepper before grilling means that you will quickly get a brown top without the cheese melting off the pineapple and ham. If you are extra hungry, toast a split bap and top each half bap with ham and pineapple and cheese.

CHICKEN

Chicken in Lemon Mayonnaise
(for six)

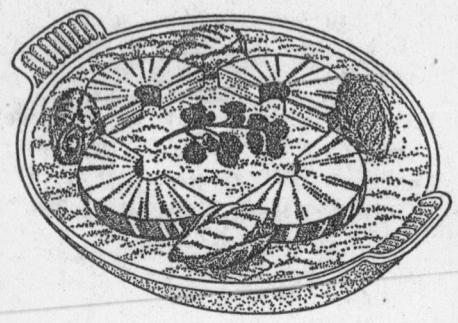

3 lb cooked chicken
1 small fresh pineapple
juice of 1 lemon
½ pint thick home-made or good bought mayonnaise
salt and pepper
1 oz walnuts, chopped
lettuce hearts and watercress to garnish

Remove the meat from chicken. Slice white meat and cut dark meat into bite-sized pieces.

Slice the pineapple and remove skin and centre core. Cut three slices in half and reserve them for the garnish. Chop the remaining pineapple.

Stir the lemon juice into the mayonnaise and season to taste. Mix 3 to 4 tablespoons of mayonnaise with the dark chicken meat and arrange it on a serving dish. Cover with the chopped pineapple. Lay slices of white meat on top and coat with remaining mayonnaise.

Sprinkle over the chopped walnuts and garnish the dish with lettuce hearts, watercress and the halved slices of pineapple.

Cook's Tip This is a very good way of using up turkey after Christmas and makes a delicious special cold supper dish, when you have friends in. Canned pineapple may be used if liked but the flavour is rather sweeter than using fresh pineapple. If preparing ahead, mix lemon mayonnaise with the two different coloured meats and put in plastic containers. Prepare pineapple, then assemble 30 minutes before the meal.

Chicken in Orange Cream Sauce
(for four)

1 large onion, finely chopped
$\frac{3}{4}$ oz butter
1 tablespoon oil
$\frac{1}{2}$ can concentrated frozen orange juice (3 fl. oz)
$\frac{1}{4}$ pint home-made stock *or*
1 chicken stock cube dissolved in
$\frac{1}{4}$ pint water
4 sprigs of fresh tarragon, chopped *or*
1 tablespoon dried tarragon
4 chicken quarters
salt and pepper
$\frac{1}{2}$ oz cornflour mixed with 2 tablespoons cold water
5 oz soured cream

Fry onion gently in butter and oil for 3 minutes, stirring occasionally. Add enough water to the orange juice to make it up to $\frac{1}{4}$ pint. Add orange juice, stock and tarragon to onion and stir well. Bring sauce to the boil, cover pan and simmer for 30 minutes.

Meanwhile, season chicken quarters and grill them on both sides until cooked through.

Skim any excess fat from the sauce. Stir in cornflour and bring sauce to the boil. Cook for 2 to 3 minutes, stirring constantly. Remove pan from the heat and allow sauce to cool slightly. Then stir in soured cream and any juices from the grill pan.

Transfer the grilled chicken quarters to a serving dish and pour over the sauce.

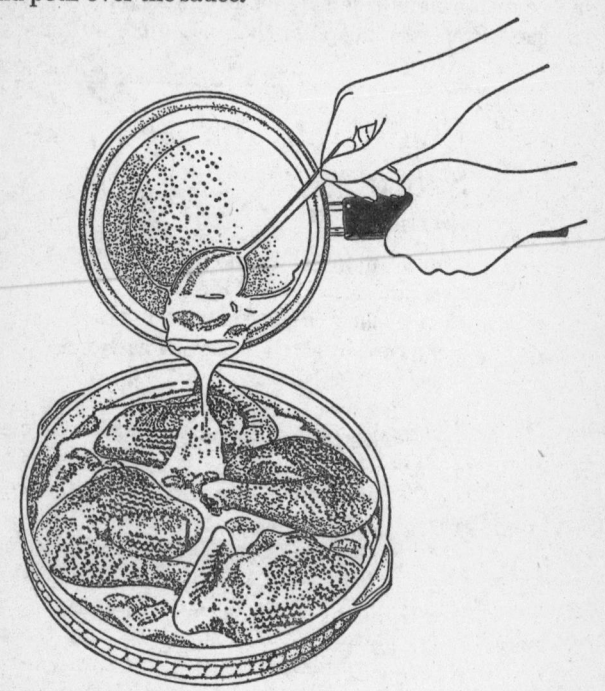

Cook's Tip Frozen concentrated orange juice is excellent for cooking and inexpensive when you think that each 6 fl. oz can contains the concentrated juice of eleven oranges. Use the remainder of the can left from this recipe to add to fruit salad or dilute as a drink.

Country Chicken Pie

(for six)

- 3 lb roasting chicken, cleaned (giblets reserved)
- 1 onion, quartered
- 1 carrot, quartered
- 1 bayleaf
- 1 sprig of fresh thyme *or* ½ teaspoon dried thyme
- 6 peppercorns
- ½ teaspoon salt
- 1½ pints water
- 3 to 4 streaky bacon rashers
- 4 oz chicken livers, each sliced in three
- 1½ oz butter
- 1 oz flour
- 4 oz mushrooms, sliced
- 1 teaspoon chopped chives
- 13 oz packet frozen puff pastry, thawed
- 1 egg, beaten with ½ teaspoon water, *or* use milk for glazing

Put the chicken and giblets (except the liver) in a saucepan with onion, carrot, herbs, seasoning and water. Cover and simmer for 1 hour or until the chicken is tender when pierced with a fork.

Remove chicken from the pan and set it aside to cool. Boil cooking liquid until it has been reduced to ½ pint. Strain cooking liquid and set aside.

Cut each bacon rasher in half, roll them up and thread on a skewer. Grill bacon rolls until fat is just transparent, turning once. Remove from heat, slide them off the skewer and set aside.

Fry chicken livers in butter for 3 minutes, stirring frequently. Remove them from the pan and chop them coarsely. Set aside.

Blend flour into butter remaining in pan and cook, stir-

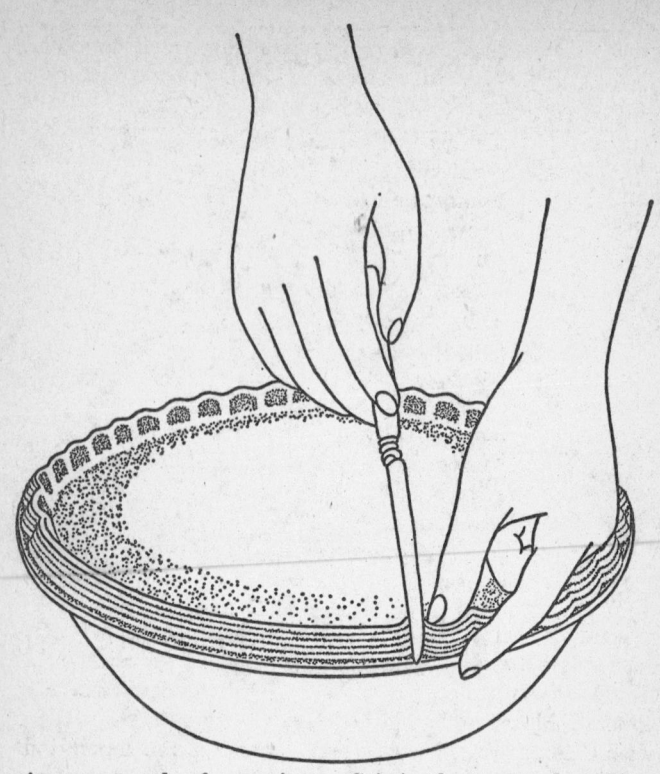

ring constantly, for 1 minute, Stir in the reserved cooking liquid. Bring sauce to the boil, still stirring, and simmer for 3 minutes.

Remove chicken meat from the bones and add it to the sauce with chicken livers, bacon rolls, mushrooms and chives. Taste sauce for seasoning and transfer mixture to a 2 pint pie dish. Set aside to cool completely.

Roll out pastry and cover dish with it in the usual way. Flute edges and, if you like, use trimmings to make a decoration for the top. Brush top of pie with egg and water or just milk and place it in the centre of the oven preheated to 425 deg. F., gas no. 7. Bake for 30 to 40 minutes or until pastry is well risen and golden brown. Serve hot.

Cook's Tip Bacon and chicken go very well together. This pie has bacon rolls in, but if there are the ends of a bacon joint to use up, cut into cubes and add them.

Sicilian Chicken
(for four)

4 chicken quarters
2 tablespoons oil
3 Spanish onions, sliced
1 garlic clove, crushed
¼ pint home-made stock *or*
1 chicken stock cube dissolved in
¼ pint water
1 teaspoon dried mixed herbs
salt and pepper
1 lb ripe tomatoes, peeled and sliced
16 Spanish stuffed green olives
1 tablespoon cornflour mixed with
    1 tablespoon cold water (optional)

Fry chicken quarters in oil until they are golden brown on both sides. Remove them from the pan and set aside. Add onions and garlic to pan and fry for 3 minutes, stirring occasionally.

Skin chicken quarters if liked, then return chicken to pan. Add stock, herbs, seasoning and sliced tomatoes. Cover pan and simmer for 30 minutes or until chicken quarters are tender when pierced with the point of a sharp knife.

Transfer chicken to a serving dish. Stir olives into sauce and pour it over chicken. If you prefer a thicker sauce, stir in cornflour, bring the sauce to the boil and simmer for 3 minutes before adding olives.

Cook's Tip Remember if using a frozen chicken or frozen chicken joints to thaw completely before cooking. The best place to do this is in the refrigerator and preferably slowly overnight.

Chicken with Cider and Mushroom Sauce

(for four)

4 chicken joints
scant ½ pint cider (sweet)
1 oz butter
1 tablespoon oil
½ lb button mushrooms
1 oz flour
pinch dried mixed herbs
5 oz carton yogurt
salt and pepper

Place the chicken joints in the cider in a casserole and bake in a preheated oven 375 deg. F., or gas no. 5, for 50 minutes. Strain off the liquid and keep chicken hot. Skin chicken if liked. Melt butter and oil, fry mushrooms for a few minutes. Add flour and cook for 1 minute. Slowly add cider and chicken juices, allowing sauce to thicken. Add mixed herbs, yogurt and seasoning. Pour over chicken to serve

Cook's Tip Using yogurt in savoury dishes instead of cream cuts down the calorie content and makes the dish less rich. It is best to blend the yogurt well before adding to the sauce to give a smooth texture. This is a generous amount of sauce and is best served with something to sop up the flavours, such as creamed potatoes or noodles.

Poule Au Pot Au Citron

(for six to eight)

4 lb boiling fowl with giblets
thinly peeled rind of 2 lemons
2 parsley sprigs
2 onions, quartered
1 carrot, quartered
bouquet garni
salt and pepper
Sauce:
2 oz butter
2 oz flour
½ pint milk
juice of 2 lemons
chopped fresh parsley to garnish

Rinse fowl with cold water. Put giblets, the rind of half a lemon and a sprig of parsley inside bird. Secure legs with a skewer or string. Put bird in a saucepan with the rest of lemon rind and second parsley sprig, onions, carrot, bouquet garni and seasoning. Pour in enough water to cover and bring to the boil. Simmer for 2 to 4 hours, depending on the age of the bird, or until it is tender. To test, remove string or skewer and raise drumstick to see if joint of leg is loose.

Remove the bird from saucepan and discard giblets, lemon rind and parsley inside. Set aside on a serving dish and keep hot while you make the sauce.

Skim the fat off stock in the saucepan and strain off half a pint. Set aside (the remainder can be used for soup). In another saucepan, melt butter and stir in flour. Cook this roux over low heat for 2 minutes, stirring constantly. Remove pan from the heat and gradually add milk, stirring constantly, add reserved stock. Return pan to the heat and bring sauce to the boil, still stirring. Simmer until sauce has thickened, then stir in lemon juice. Taste the sauce and add more seasoning if necessary.

Pour sauce over the bird. Sprinkle with the parsley and serve.

Cook's Tip Boiling fowls have a really good flavour, no definite cooking time can be given as it depends on the age of the bird how long it will take for it to be tender. If boiling fowl is not available use a roasting chicken and cook until just tender.

Herby Chicken and Ham Pie

(for four)

1 knuckle of ham or bacon
1½ oz butter
1 large onion, sliced
1 oz flour
¼ pint milk
¼ pint chicken stock *or*
1 chicken stock cube dissolved in
¼ pint water
1 level teaspoon mixed herbs
½ level teaspoon salt
pepper
about 6 oz cooked chicken meat, diced
Pastry:
8 oz plain flour
good pinch salt
2 oz margarine
2 oz lard or white fat
water to mix
milk to glaze

Cook knuckle slowly in a covered saucepan with just sufficient water to cover, simmer for about 1¼ to 2 hours until tender. Drain, remove skin and strip off 6 oz meat. Cut this into neat cubes. Melt butter in a saucepan and fry onion until soft but not coloured. Stir in the flour and cook for 1 minute. Gradually add milk and stock and bring to the boil, stirring frequently. Add herbs, salt and pepper and simmer for 2 minutes. Stir in ham and chopped chicken, check seasoning and leave to cool.

Sieve flour and salt into a bowl and rub in fats until mixture resembles fine breadcrumbs. Add sufficient water to mix to a pliable dough. On a lightly floured surface, roll out $\frac{2}{3}$ of the pastry and use to line an $8\frac{1}{2}$ inch shallow pie tin or dish. Spoon chicken mixture into pastry and level top. Roll out remaining pastry to make a lid. Damp edges of pie and position lid, pressing edges well together. Trim off excess pastry and crimp edges. Roll out trimmings and use to decorate top of pie. Brush pastry with milk, make a small hole in the centre and cook in preheated oven at 425 deg. F., or gas no. 7, for 20 minutes, then reduce to 350 deg. F., or gas no. 4, for a further 25 to 30 minutes until golden brown. Serve hot or cold.

Cook's Tip This chicken pie is a very good way of using up the last trimmings from a roast chicken. Include the cooked liver, too, if it hasn't been used in the stuffing. If there isn't quite enough of the chicken left, add a few pieces of chopped cooked root vegetables such as carrots and celery.

Chicken and Liver Terrine
(for four to six)

¾ lb liver (lambs' or pigs')
10 oz streaky bacon rashers, de-rinded
1 large onion
2 cloves garlic
1½ level teaspoons salt
plenty of pepper
¼ level teaspoon ground nutmeg
8 pimento stuffed olives, chopped
1 egg, beaten
2 tablespoons sherry
1 large raw chicken portion
few extra pimento stuffed olives
watercress

Put liver, 4 oz bacon, onion and garlic through the fine blade of a mincer. Add salt, pepper, nutmeg, olives, egg and sherry and mix well. Strip flesh from the chicken portion, discard skin, and cut into narrow strips. Stretch remaining bacon rashers with the back of a knife then use to line a medium sized loaf tin (approx 7"×5"). Spoon in

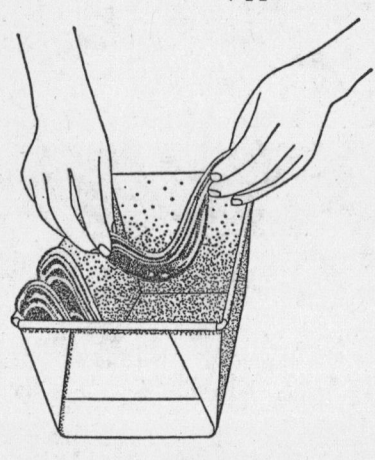

half liver mixture, cover with pieces of raw chicken and spoon remaining liver on top. Fold over ends of bacon. Stand the tin in a baking tin containing 1 inch hot water and cook in oven preheated to 300 deg. F., or gas no. 2, for $2\frac{1}{4}$ hours. Remove from the baking tin and cool slightly. Cover with greaseproof paper and weights. Cool and then chill for several hours. Turn out and serve garnished with sliced olives and watercress.

Cook's Tip This terrine can be served as a starter to serve 8 to 10 portions, as a main course or as part of a cold buffet with salads, and is also ideal for picnics. It will freeze well for up to 3 months.

Savoury Stuffed Pancakes
(makes about 8 pancakes)

Batter:
4 oz flour
$\frac{1}{4}$ teaspoon salt
1 egg
$\frac{1}{2}$ pint milk
1 tablespoon salad oil
oil for frying
Filling:
8 oz cooked chicken, diced
$10\frac{1}{2}$ oz can condensed mushroom soup
1 dessertspoon chopped parsley
salt and pepper
4 oz grated cheese

Make the batter in the usual way (see recipe for Lemon Pancakes, page 106) and make about 8 pancakes, using a 7 or 8 inch frying pan. Stack pancakes, with a piece of greaseproof paper between each, and set aside.

Mix together chicken, mushroom soup, parsley and seasoning to taste. Spread out pancakes on a flat surface, spoon some of the chicken filling on to each, and roll them up. Arrange rolled-up pancakes on a flat, ovenproof dish and sprinkle with cheese.

Bake in the oven preheated to 400 deg. F., or gas no. 6, for 20 to 25 minutes or until the pancakes are heated through and the cheese is golden brown.

Cook's Tip Batter keeps for 2 days in the refrigerator, so if you make twice the amount, the next lot could be used for toad-in-the-hole or Yorkshire pudding.

EGGS

Soft-Boiled Eggs in Onion Sauce
(for four)

½ lb small onions
½ pint milk
8 eggs
1½ oz butter
1½ oz flour
salt and pepper
paprika pepper
French bread

Peel onions, place in a small saucepan, cover with water and simmer until tender, about 20 minutes. Drain ¼ pint of onion water from the pan and mix with milk. Roughly chop onions. Cook eggs in boiling water for 4 minutes, plunge into cold water, leave to cool, then carefully crack the shells and peel. Arrange in an ovenproof serving dish. Melt butter in a small pan, stir in flour and cook for 2 to 3 minutes, add milk and onion water mixture and bring to the boil stirring. Add chopped onion, season to taste and cook gently for 5 minutes. Spoon sauce over the eggs and place in a moderate oven for about 10 minutes to heat through. Sprinkle with paprika pepper and serve.

Cook's Tip Not a dish usually favoured by men, but ideal for lunch when he's out! Serve with mashed potatoes or French bread to sop up the sauce. Take care not to overcook the eggs as the joy of this dish is to have nice runny centres to the eggs.

Supper Baked Eggs
(for two)

2 rashers back bacon
2 tomatoes
4 mushrooms
butter
2 eggs

Remove rind and any bone from the bacon and cut each rasher in half. Halve tomatoes. Place two pieces of bacon and two tomatoes and mushrooms in two small ovenproof dishes. Place a knob of butter on top of each mushroom and bake in the centre of a moderately hot oven, preheated to 400 deg. F., or gas no. 6, for about 10 minutes. Crack an egg into the centre of each dish and bake for a further 5 minutes. Serve at once with garlic rolls.

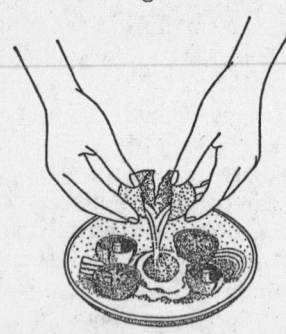

Garlic Rolls
(for two)

½ small clove of garlic
a little salt
freshly ground black pepper
2 crisp white bread rolls
1 oz butter

Peel the garlic and crush to a smooth paste with salt.
Cream butter until soft and beat in garlic and black pepper.
Make two cuts an inch apart through each roll to within
½ inch of the base. Spread with butter. Bake in a hot oven
pre-heated to 400 deg. F., or gas no. 6, for 15 minutes
wrapped in foil.

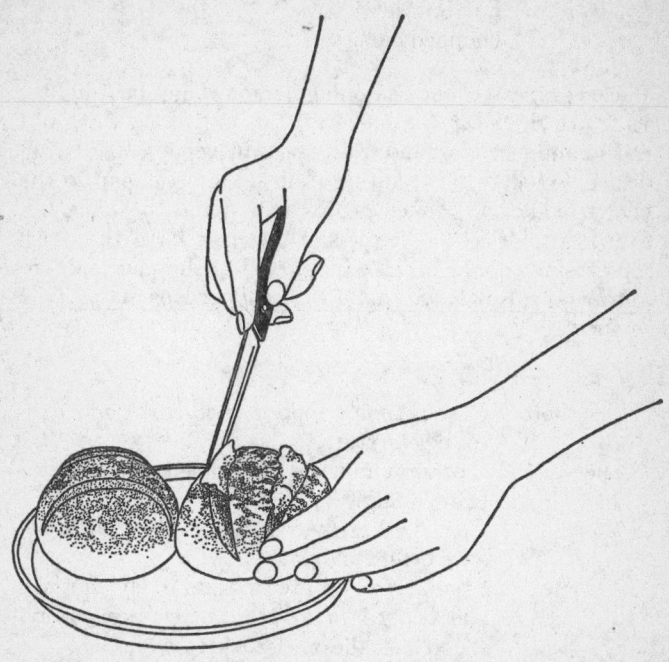

Cook's Tip Make garlic bread, too, by the same method,
only treble the quantity for a small French loaf. Garlic
butter keeps if tightly covered in the refrigerator, and is
also delicious served on grilled chops and steaks.

Omelettes

(for one)

2 eggs
1 tablespoon water
salt and pepper
½ oz butter
chopped parsley

Place eggs, water and seasoning in a bowl and beat lightly with a fork. Heat the omelette pan until very hot, add butter and when hot and frothy pour in egg mixture. Using a fork, quickly draw mixture from sides of the pan to the centre to allow uncooked egg to run underneath, shake pan and leave for a few seconds. Draw pan from the heat, loosen sides, fold omelette in three, tap the pan and slip onto a warm plate. Sprinkle with chopped parsley. Serve at once.

Fillings:

Fine herbs: 1 tablespoon chopped fresh herbs added to the egg mixture.

Cheese: 1 oz grated cheese sprinkled on omelette before folding.

Ham: 1 oz diced cooked ham, sprinkled on omelette before folding.

Tomato: 1 tomato, peeled, seeded and finely chopped and cooked in a little butter. Season and spoon onto the omelette before folding.

Mushroom: Quarter 1 to 2 oz small mushrooms and sauté in butter for 5 minutes, season and spoon onto the omelette before folding.

Spanish: Peel and finely dice a small onion, seed and finely shred half a small green pepper. Cook in a little butter or oil for 5 minutes. Stir in a peeled and sliced tomato. Stir into the egg mixture and make the omelette as usual, but do not fold, slip flat onto a plate.

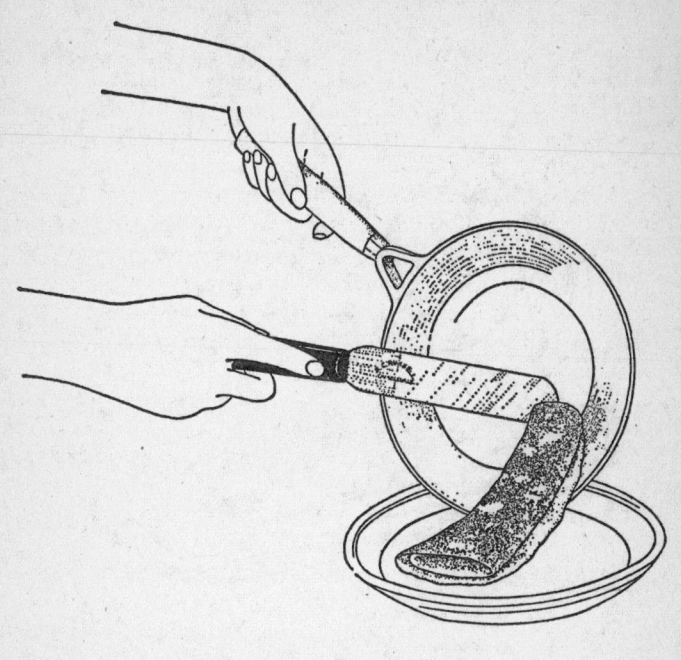

Cook's Tip To make the Classic French omelette you must get the pan very hot before adding the butter. Then work quickly when the egg mixture goes into the pan (see basic recipe). The centre of the omelette should be hardly set when served.

FISH

Jugged Kippers
(for one)

1 whole kipper

To avoid cooking smells, one of the best ways to cook kippers is to place the kipper fillets in a jug or shallow dish and pour boiling water over them. Cover the jug or dish with a lid, or plate, or with foil. Leave without further heating for 5 minutes. Drain off the water and you will find the kippers cooked to perfection.

Cook's Tip Sometimes a large kipper or a packet of kipper fillets is too much for one meal. Any left-overs can be flaked, kept cool and covered, and used the next day for Kipper Scramble.

Kipper Scramble
(for one)

1 kipper fillet
2 standard eggs
pepper
a knob of butter or margarine
a slice of buttered toast

After cooking the kipper (see page 72) remove skin and flake fish while it is still warm. Beat eggs, season with pepper but not salt, and add flaked kipper. Melt knob of butter in saucepan, pour in egg mixture. Keep heat low. Stir mixture continuously until eggs are creamy and soft. Remove from heat just before mixture looks fully set as cooking continues in the heat of the pan. Serve at once on buttered toast.

Cook's Tip This is a good way of introducing children to kippers.

Tuna Spaghetti Bake
(for four)

8 oz spaghetti
salt and pepper
2½ oz butter
2 oz flour
1 pint milk
½ level teaspoon made mustard
4 oz Cheddar cheese, grated
1 large onion, sliced
7 oz can tunafish, drained and roughly flaked
2 hard-boiled eggs, roughly chopped
1 level teaspoon chopped basil

Cook spaghetti in boiling, salted water until almost tender – about 10 minutes. Drain very well and rinse. Melt 2 oz butter in a saucepan then stir in the flour and cook for 1 minute. Gradually add milk and bring to the boil, stirring frequently. Add 1 level teaspoon salt, pepper to taste and the mustard and simmer for 2 minutes. Remove from heat and stir in 3 oz cheese until melted. Fry onion in the remaining butter until golden brown, then drain. Lightly grease a 3 pint casserole and place half the spaghetti in the bottom. Pour over half the sauce. Cover with the tunafish,

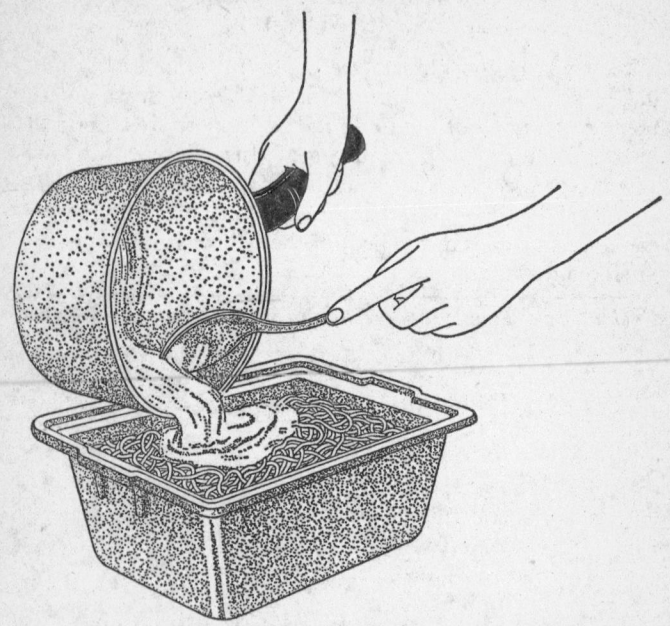

then the chopped eggs and cooked onions. Finally sprinkle with the basil. Lay remaining spaghetti on top then pour the rest of the sauce over it. Sprinkle top with remaining cheese. Cook in preheated oven at 400 deg. F., or gas no. 6, for about 45 minutes until the top is well browned.

Cook's Tip This dish can be prepared in advance, cooled and chilled in the refrigerator for 1 or 2 days and then reheated when required as above, but cooking time increased to 1 hour.

salads and vegetables

SALADS

Coleslaw Salad
(for six)

1 small, hard, white cabbage, weighing about 1½ lb
½ pint French dressing
salt and pepper
1 small onion
2 carrots
⅛ pint mayonnaise

Cut cabbage into 4 and trim away hard stalk, then finely slice into strips. Place in a mixing bowl with French dressing (see page 79), seasoning and very finely chopped onion. Toss well, cover and leave in the refrigerator overnight. Next day, grate the carrots coarsely and stir in with the mayonnaise. Leave to stand for an hour before serving. Pile into a serving dish and serve sprinkled with paprika pepper.

Cook's Tip If you make coleslaw in two stages like this, it uses a lot less mayonnaise and the flavours really have a chance to blend overnight in the refrigerator. If white cabbage is not available, you can use shredded sprouts.

Curried Egg Mayonnaise
(for four)

4 hard-boiled eggs
4 tablespoons home-made mayonnaise
2 teaspoons lemon juice
1 tablespoon mango chutney juice
$\frac{1}{2}$–1 level teaspoon curry powder
salt and pepper
sprigs of cress

Cut the hard-boiled eggs lengthways in half and arrange them on a serving dish. Blend together the mayonnaise (see page 77), lemon juice, chutney juice, curry powder and seasonings. Spoon the mayonnaise over the eggs and decorate with sprigs of cress.

Cook's Tip To avoid a black ring round the edge of the yolk of a hard-boiled egg, only boil eggs for 9 to 10 minutes. Cool quickly in running water until absolutely cold.

Mayonnaise

2 egg yolks
$\frac{1}{2}$ level teaspoon made mustard
$\frac{1}{2}$ level teaspoon salt
$\frac{1}{8}$ level teaspoon pepper
$\frac{1}{2}$ level teaspoon caster sugar
1 tablespoon white wine vinegar *or* distilled malt vinegar
$\frac{1}{2}$ pint olive, vegetable *or* corn oil
1 tablespoon lemon juice

Stand a bowl on a damp cloth to prevent it slipping on the table. Put egg yolks, mustard, salt, pepper, sugar and vinegar into the bowl and mix thoroughly. Add the oil drop by drop, beating well with a whisk the whole time until sauce is thick and smooth. Then beat in lemon juice. (In order that the oil may be added a drop at a time, put into the bottle neck a cork from which a small wedge has been cut.) This makes a traditional thick mayonnaise. For a thinner mixture, add a little cream or top of the milk.

Cook's Tip Should the sauce curdle because the oil has been added too quickly to the egg yolks, take a fresh yolk and start again, adding the curdled mayonnaise very slowly to it in the same way as the oil was added to the original egg yolks.

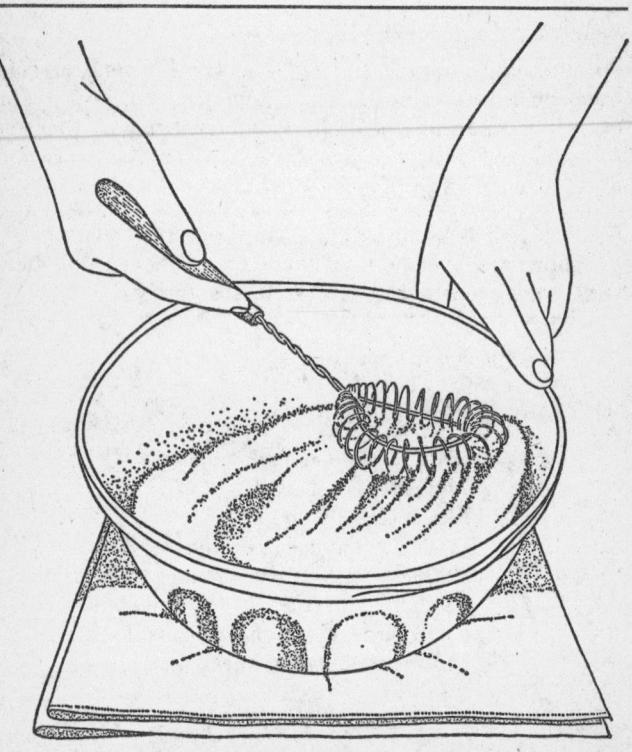

French Dressing

- ½ clove garlic, crushed
- ½–1 level teaspoon salt
- ¼–½ level teaspoon freshly ground black pepper
- 1 level teaspoon very finely chopped onion *or* some finely chopped chives
- 1 level teaspoon caster sugar
- ¼ pint olive, vegetable *or* corn oil
- 4 to 6 tablespoons cider *or* white wine vinegar (if not available, use distilled malt vinegar)
- ½ level teaspoon dry mustard

Blend all the ingredients together.

Cook's Tip In summer make four times this recipe and keep in a bottle in a cool place ready to use for salads. Give the bottle a good shake before using each time.

VEGETABLES

Stuffed Red Peppers With Cheese Sauce
(for six)

4 shallots, chopped
1 lb raw minced beef
2 rounded tablespoons flour
½ pint home-made stock *or*
1 beef stock cube dissolved in
½ pint water
2 carrots, coarsely grated
salt and pepper
6 small red peppers

Cheese sauce:

1 oz butter
1 oz flour
½ pint milk
½ teaspoon made mustard
2 oz grated cheese
salt and pepper

Fry shallots and minced beef together for 5 minutes, stirring frequently. Stir in flour and then stock. Bring to the boil. Add carrots and seasoning to taste. Cover pan, reduce the heat and simmer for 30 minutes.

Meanwhile, cut stalk and core out of top of peppers and shake out seeds. Blanch peppers in boiling water for 5 minutes. Drain well and set aside.

To make cheese sauce: melt butter in a saucepan and stir in flour. Cook, stirring constantly, for 2 minutes. Remove pan from the heat and gradually stir in milk. Return pan to the heat. Bring to the boil and simmer, stirring for 3 minutes. Stir in mustard, cheese and seasoning to taste. Remove the pan from the heat, cover, and set aside.

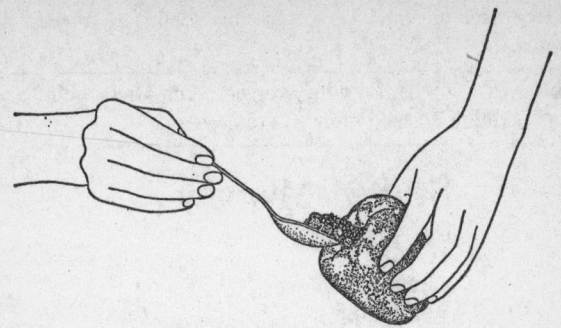

Now fill each pepper with the minced beef mixture. Place them in a shallow ovenproof serving dish and pour cheese sauce around them. Put dish in the oven preheated to 350 deg. F., or gas no. 4, and bake for 25 minutes. Serve hot with French bread or soft rolls.

Cook's Tip For this recipe you can use small frozen peppers, one per person, if already seeded before freezing. It is sufficient to partly thaw before filling. No need in any case to blanch frozen peppers.

Stuffed Tomatoes
(for four)

8 large tomatoes
8 oz cream cheese
4 oz cooked ham, finely diced
salt and pepper
1 dessertspoon chopped chives
watercress to garnish

Cut a thin slice from base of each tomato, carefully scoop out pulp inside and reserve.

Cream the cheese with a wooden spoon until it is soft. Mix in ham and 3 tablespoons of tomato pulp. Season well and add chives. Fill tomatoes with cheese and ham mixture. Replace tomato slices on top, like a cap. Garnish with watercress and serve with bread or crispbread and butter.

Cook's Tip   For those who are watching their weight, use cottage cheese instead of cream cheese.

Stuffed Marrow
(for four to six)

2 large onions
½ oz dripping
1 lb raw minced beef
¼ pint home-made stock *or*
½ stock cube dissolved in
¼ pint water
salt and pepper
gravy browning
¾ lb tomatoes
4 oz fresh white breadcrumbs
1 medium sized marrow (about 3 lb)

Finely chop the onions. Melt dripping in a pan, add the mince and onions and fry for 5 minutes. Stir in stock, seasoning and a little gravy browning. Skin the tomatoes, slice one and reserve for garnish; quarter the remainder and add to the pan. Cover and cook for 30 minutes.

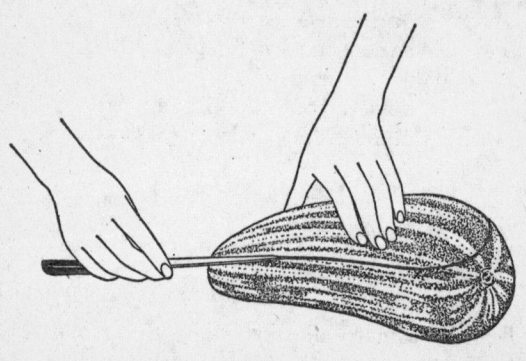

Remove the mince from the heat and stir in the breadcrumbs to thicken, add more seasoning if necessary.

Cut an oval shaped lid from one side of the marrow and scoop out all the seeds. Fill the centre of the marrow with the mince mixture and lay the sliced tomato on top. Place back the lid and wrap the marrow in lightly buttered foil.

Bake in a moderate oven preheated to 350 deg. F., or gas no. 4, for about 1 hour or until tender.

Cook's Tip Use a young marrow for this recipe if possible. If you can't easily break the skin with your thumb-nail, peel the marrow with a potato peeler before stuffing.

Summer Vegetables au Gratin
(for four to six)

8 oz new carrots, cut into even lengths
½ small cauliflower, broken into flowerets
4 oz French beans, trimmed
8 oz courgettes, sliced
1 oz fresh white breadcrumbs
2 tablespoons salad oil
1 oz butter
salt and pepper
Cheese sauce:
1 oz butter
1 oz flour
¼ pint milk
1 teaspoon made mustard
4 oz grated cheese
salt and pepper

Cook carrots in boiling salted water for 5 minutes. Add cauliflower and beans and cook for a further 5 minutes. Add courgettes and cook for 3 minutes.

While the vegetables are cooking. fry breadcrumbs in oil and butter until they are brown, stirring frequently.

Season the breadcrumbs and remove pan from heat. Keep hot.

Drain vegetables, reserving $\frac{1}{4}$ pint of the vegetable water. Place vegetables in a warmed dish and keep hot.

To make the sauce: melt butter in a saucepan, and stir in flour. Cook, stirring constantly, for 2 minutes. Remove the pan from the heat and gradually stir in milk and vegetable water. Return pan to the heat. Bring to the boil and simmer, stirring, for 3 minutes. Stir in mustard, cheese and seasoning.

Pour the sauce over the vegetables, sprinkle with breadcrumbs. Serve hot.

Cook's Tip Vary the vegetables according to season. Just cook them until barely tender before adding the cheese sauce.

Leek and Tomato Flan

(for four to six)

$1\frac{1}{2}$ lb leeks
2 oz butter
$7\frac{1}{2}$ oz packet frozen puff pastry, thawed
1 tablespoon chopped fresh herbs
6 to 8 slices Cheddar cheese
2 tomatoes, sliced

Wash leeks and thinly slice white part only. Fry very gently in butter for 20 minutes, stirring occasionally.

Meanwhile, roll out pastry dough and line a shallow Swiss roll tin $11'' \times 7''$. Drain leeks on kitchen paper towels and spread them over base of pastry case. Sprinkle them with herbs and cover with slices of cheese. Place tomato slices on top. Put flan in the oven preheated to 425 deg. F., or gas no. 7, and bake for 15 to 20 minutes, or until pastry is cooked and the cheese is a light golden brown. Serve warm or cold with a green salad.

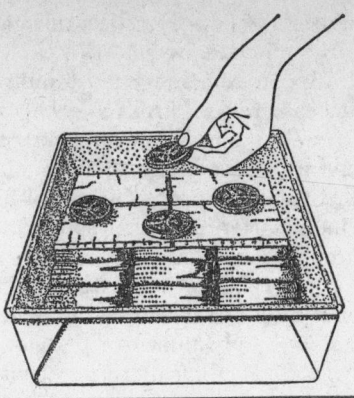

Cook's Tip Using a metal tin to cook flans means that you get a really crisp underneath to the pastry.

Baked Onions
(for four)

4 large onions *or*
8 medium sized onions, peeled
1 tablespoon dripping
1 lb raw minced beef
2 large tomatoes, peeled and chopped
1 level teaspoon dried thyme or basil
1 level teaspoon salt
pepper to taste
½ teaspoon Worcester sauce
1 level teaspoon paprika
1½ oz butter
3 level tablespoons flour
½ pint milk

Place onions in a saucepan. Barely cover with water and bring to the boil. Cover pan and simmer for 25 minutes. Drain onions and reserve ¼ pint liquor. Remove the centres carefully. Melt the dripping and fry mince gently for 5 to 10 minutes, stirring frequently. Add tomatoes, thyme, salt and pepper, Worcester sauce and paprika and continue cooking for 3 to 4 minutes. Spoon meat carefully into the onion cavities. Spoon remaining meat mixture into the base of a 4 pint casserole or a foil-lined baking tin. Stand the onions on top. Cover casserole or enclose the onions in a foil parcel and cook in a preheated oven at 350 deg. F., or gas no. 4, for 1 to 1½ hours or until onions are tender.

Meanwhile melt butter in a pan. Chop onion centres and fry gently in the butter for 10 minutes, without colouring. Stir in the flour and cook for 1 minute then gradually add onion liquor and milk and bring to the boil, stirring frequently. Season well and simmer for 3 minutes. Serve the onions on a spoonful of meat mixture with the sauce handed separately.

Cook's Tip If peeling onions always makes you cry, try peeling them under water. For chopping several onions wear sunglasses to help keep the juices from stinging your eyes.

Red Cabbage
(for four)

1 medium red cabbage
1 lb windfall apples, weight after peeling
¼ pint water
1½ oz sugar
1 teaspoon salt
4 cloves
6 tablespoons vinegar
2 oz butter
1 tablespoon redcurrant jelly

Trim and clean cabbage. Shred finely. Peel, core and slice apples. Place cabbage and apples in a pan with the water, sugar, salt and cloves. Cover, simmer until tender, about ¾ hour. Remove cloves, add vinegar, butter and jelly. Blend well over the heat. Check seasoning and serve hot with meat dishes.

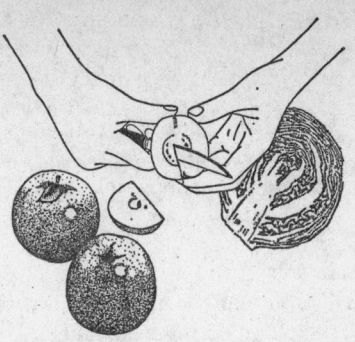

Cook's Tip One of the best and most warming vegetables, it also reheats well, should some be left. Reheat in a non-stick pan, stirring until piping hot.

Potato and Onion Bake
(for four)

2 oz butter
2 onions, thinly sliced
1¾ lb potatoes, thinly sliced
salt and pepper
parsley to garnish

Melt butter in a frying pan and fry onions for 4 minutes, stirring occasionally. With a slotted spoon, transfer onions to a shallow 2 pint ovenproof dish. Arrange potato slices on top of onions and pour over butter remaining in frying pan.

Season well and cover dish tightly with aluminium foil. Place the dish in the oven preheated to 350 deg. F., or gas no. 4, and cook for 30 minutes. Remove foil and continue cooking for a further 30 minutes.

Garnish with the parsley and serve.

Cook's Tip If preparing the potato slices ahead for this recipe, leave them soaking in cold water for up to 12 hours. The onions too may be sliced, covered and kept cool.

Rosti

(for four)

2 lb large potatoes, scrubbed
½ teaspoon salt
4 tablespoons salad oil
1 oz butter

Boil potatoes in salted water for 10 to 15 minutes or until the point of a knife can be inserted into the potato for about 1 inch before meeting resistance. Drain potatoes, and when cooler, peel. Leave potatoes to become completely cold, then grate coarsely. Toss in salt. Melt half the oil and butter in pan, preferably a non-stick pan. Add potato and flatten with a fish slice. Fry over a low heat for about 30 minutes. Check, using a fish slice to lift the sides up – when pale golden brown the underside is done. Turn out onto a large plate. Put remainder of oil and butter in pan and heat. Slide potato cake off plate into the hot fat and brown second side.

Serve at once. Fried onions and bacon are often served in the Rosti. They should be sandwiched in the potato as it is put in the frying pan.

Cook's Tip The Swiss variation on fried potato. The great secret is to fry very slowly so that the Rosti potato cake is crispy brown on both sides. A good base for a supper dish.

---

puddings hot and cold

COLD

Midsummer Pudding
(for four to six)

6 to 8 large slices of white bread
$\frac{3}{4}$ lb rhubarb
$\frac{1}{2}$ lb blackcurrants
$\frac{1}{2}$ lb granulated sugar
6 tablespoons water
$\frac{1}{2}$ lb strawberries
$\frac{1}{4}$ lb raspberries

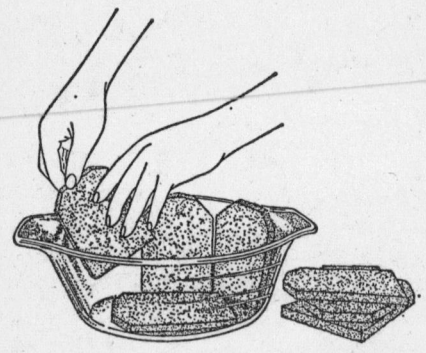

Cut crusts from the bread and put aside 1 slice for the top. Use remainder of bread to line base and sides of a 2 pint, round, fairly shallow dish. Cut rhubarb into $\frac{1}{2}$ inch slices and put with blackcurrants in a saucepan. Add the sugar and water and bring to the boil. Simmer until barely tender, stirring, this will only take a few minutes. Add strawberries and raspberries and cook for a further minute.

Turn mixture into prepared dish, place slice of bread on top and bend over top of sliced bread at the sides towards centre. Put a saucer on top pressing down a little until the juice rises to the top of the dish. Leave to soak until cold or overnight in refrigerator. Turn out just before serving and serve with lots of cream.

Cook's Tip The very same fruit filling for midsummer pudding can be served on its own with fresh cream as a rich red fruit salad. If you find that the suggested fruits are not available, substitute others. Loganberries and other currants may be used with either fresh or frozen fruit. Midsummer pudding must be served chilled.

Gooseberry Fool
(for six)

1 lb gooseberries
2 tablespoons water
3 to 4 oz caster sugar
½ pint plain yogurt (p. 99)
½ pint fairly thick cold custard
a little green colouring
sponge finger biscuits

Place gooseberries in a saucepan with water and cook gently until tender, about 15 minutes. Sieve the gooseberries into a large bowl and add sugar to taste. Leave to become quite cold. Stir yogurt with custard using a whisk, add gooseberry purée and, if liked, a few drops of

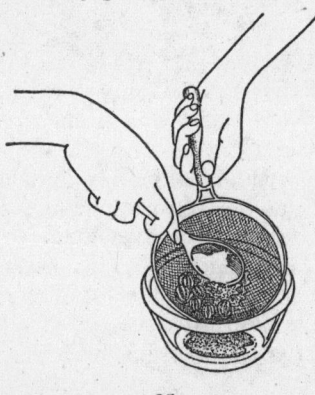

green colouring. Turn into 6 individual glass serving dishes. Chill thoroughly and serve with sponge biscuits.

Cook's Tip   Fresh or frozen gooseberries may be used. For special occasions use less custard and instead add whipped cream.

Ginger and Sherry Dessert
(for four)

¼ pint double cream
¼ pint single cream
8 oz ginger biscuits
½ glass cooking sherry
Crystallised *or* stem ginger *or* maraschino cherries for decoration

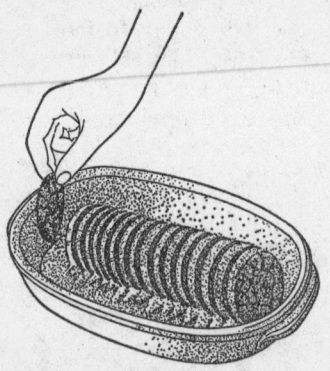

Place half the double and half single cream in a bowl and whisk together until fairly stiff peaks are formed. Dip ginger biscuits quickly in sherry, then use cream to sandwich the ginger biscuits together into a long roll. Arrange on a serving dish and leave in refrigerator or a cool place overnight. Next day, whisk the remaining creams together and use to cover the ginger biscuit roll completely. Decorate the roll with small pieces of crystallised or stem ginger or maraschino cherries. To serve cut in slices at a slight angle so that a stripey effect is achieved.

Cook's Tip An instant pudding which must be partly made the day before so that the ginger biscuits become soft and spongey. More suitable for grown-ups than children.

Helen's Chocolate Cream Layer Pudding
(for four)

4 rounded tablespoons drinking chocolate
1 level tablespoon coffee powder
4 oz fresh white breadcrumbs
4 oz demerara sugar
¼ pint double cream
¼ pint single cream
chocolate flake bar

Place chocolate, coffee powder, breadcrumbs and sugar together in a bowl and mix thoroughly. Put single and double cream together in another bowl and whisk until thick and soft peaks are formed when the whisk is lifted out. Starting with chocolate mixture, layer with whipped cream in a serving dish, finishing with a layer of cream. Leave in a cool place for at least 8 to 10 hours before serving. This pudding may be made a day in advance. Before serving, decorate with pieces of chocolate flake.

Cook's Tip A very good way of using up bread in the form of crumbs. This is not a cheap pudding to make but it is delicious. The easiest way to make breadcrumbs is with fresh bread in an electric blender but if you haven't one use 2 to 3 day-old bread and grate it on a grater or rub through a coarse sieve.

Barbados Cream
(for six)

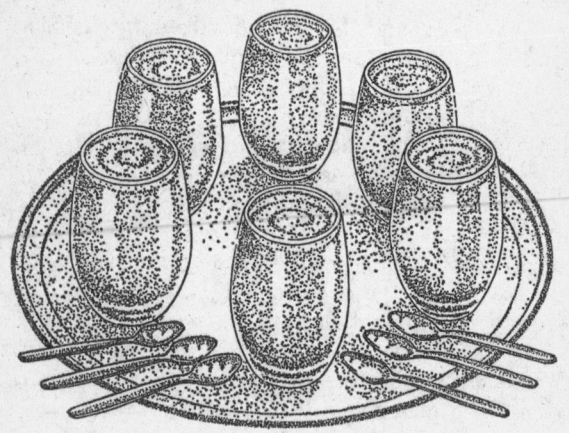

¼ pint double cream, lightly whipped
1 pint plain yogurt
soft dark brown sugar

Blend cream, add yogurt, put in 1½ pint glass dish, or in 6 small glasses. Sprinkle with ¼ inch layer of sugar. Put in refrigerator overnight. Sprinkle again with sugar before serving chilled.

Cook's Tip This is a special recipe of our producer on 'Good Afternoon'. I think it is best served in small glasses or dishes so that as you stir the cream while eating, the rich brown topping blends in thick threads.

Syllabub
(for four)

1 large lemon
4 tablespoons fairly sweet sherry
2 tablespoons brandy
2 oz caster sugar
½ pint double cream
lemon slices to decorate

Squeeze juice from lemon. Put juice in a bowl with sherry and brandy, add sugar and stir until dissolved. Pour in the cream and whisk the mixture until it forms soft peaks when the whisk is lifted out. Spoon into individual glasses and leave in a cool place until required. Top each glass with a slice of fresh lemon. This syllabub can be made a day in advance as it keeps very well.

Cook's Tip Quite the easiest of puddings to make. Very rich and best served in individual small dishes or glasses. Or even serve in small old-fashioned coffee cups with the spoon ready in the saucer.

Meringues
(for six double meringues)

3 egg whites
6 oz caster sugar
¼ pint double cream

Line 2 baking sheets with silicone paper (see *Cook's Tip*) or lightly oiled greaseproof paper. Place egg whites in a large bowl and whisk until they form soft peaks. Add sugar a teaspoon at a time, whisking well after each addition. Fill a tablespoon with the meringue and smooth it into a mound from each side with a knife. Hold side of spoon on baking sheet and carefully scoop meringue off with another

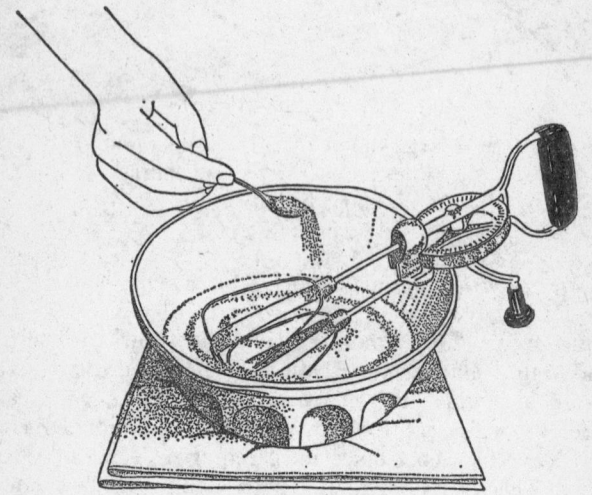

spoon. Repeat to make 12 meringue shells. Place in centre of oven preheated to 175–200 deg. F., or gas no. ¼, for 3 to 4 hours until the meringues are dry and will easily lift from silicone paper on baking sheet. Leave to cool. Whisk the cream until thick and use to sandwich the meringue shells together.

Cook's Tip Here is an absolutely foolproof way of making meringues. My secret is simple.
1. Use electric mixer or rotary whisk
2. Whisk whites until stiff
3. Add caster sugar to whites little by little, whisking all the time until sugar is incorporated, see recipe.

Silicone paper is non-stick paper especially for use with meringues. The same sheets can be used time and time again, and the surplus sugar just brushed off. Buy it from Harrods or stationers by the sheet or roll. My last packet lasted me 3 years!

Raspberry Meringue Basket
(enough for six)

3 egg whites
6 oz caster sugar
¼ pint double cream
¾ lb raspberries

Line a baking sheet with silicone paper or lightly oiled greaseproof paper. Mark an 8" circle on the paper. Place egg whites in a large bowl and whisk until they form soft peaks. Add sugar a teaspoon at a time, whisking well after each addition. Place meringue in a cloth-piping bag fitted with a large rose pipe and fill the circle with the meringue to make a flat base. Pipe rosettes of meringue around the edge to build up the sides. Bake in the centre of the oven preheated to the lowest setting 175–200 deg. F., or gas no. $\frac{1}{4}$, for 3 to 4 hours until the meringue is crisp and has dried out. Remove from the oven, leave to cool and carefully remove the paper.

One hour before serving, whisk the cream until light and whipped and fold in half the raspberries. Pile the mixture into meringue case and decorate with remaining fruit.

Cook's Tip Use a pan lid, flan ring or cake tin pressed on the silicone paper to mark a circle. No real need to pipe the meringue for this recipe if you like a more informal looking meringue. Just spread the meringue out to an 8" circle, then build up the sides of the meringue case to make a peaky wall so that the centre may be filled with fruit.

Apricot Yogurt Fool
(for four)

4 oz dried apricots
$\frac{1}{2}$ pint boiling water
4 oz sugar
$\frac{3}{4}$ pint yogurt

Soak apricots overnight in $\frac{1}{2}$ pint boiling water. Simmer with sugar till tender, purée in blender or sieve, and blend with yogurt. Pour into serving dishes and chill.

Cook's Tip All sorts of fools may be made with yogurt as a base; puréed, cooked gooseberries, apples, blackcurrants, rhubarb, and plums are some of the best. With gooseberries and blackcurrants purée in an electric blender, then sieve to remove all the seeds.

Home-Made Yogurt

1 pint milk
1 heaped tablespoon dried milk powder
 (Marvel)
2 heaped teaspoons bought yogurt
 (The Culture)

Heat milk to boiling, then cool in bowl of cold water to about 112 deg. F. – hot bath temperature. Put yogurt in bowl with milk. Stir, then whisk in dried milk. Cover, put in either a linen cupboard for 12 hours or vacuum flask for 6 hours. Or use a yogurt making kit.

Cook's Tip Home-made yogurt is far cheaper than bought. Adding milk powder gives it a firmer set. Use a new bought yogurt for every third time of using your own home-made yogurt as a culture.

Apricot and Lemon Flan
(for four to six)

4 oz plain digestive biscuits
2 oz butter
1 tablespoon demerara sugar
½ pint water
2 oz caster sugar
¾ lb apricots, halved and stoned
¼ pint double cream
6 oz can condensed milk
grated rind and juice of 2 large lemons
2 tablespoons apricot jam for glaze

Put biscuits in a polythene bag and crush them with a rolling pin. Set aside. Melt butter in a saucepan and stir in demerara sugar. Add biscuit crumbs and blend well. Turn crumb mixture into a 7 inch pie plate or flan dish and with

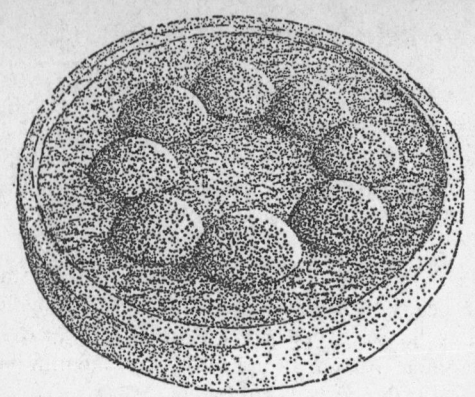

the back of a spoon, press it into shape around the base and sides. Set crumb case aside.

Put water and caster sugar in a saucepan and bring to the boil, stirring to dissolve sugar. Add apricot halves and simmer for 10 minutes or until fruit is tender. Drain fruit, reserving 2 tablespoons of cooking syrup, and leave to cool.

When apricots are cool, set 8 aside for decoration and chop remainder.

Whisk together cream, condensed milk and grated lemon rind until mixture starts to thicken. Slowly whisk in lemon juice. Fold in chopped apricots and spoon mixture into crumb case. Arrange apricot halves around the edge.

Melt apricot jam with reserved cooking syrup and use this mixture to glaze apricot halves. Chill flan for several hours before serving.

Cook's Tip In midsummer, leave out the apricots and use fresh raspberries or strawberries topped with a little melted redcurrant jelly.

Old-Fashioned Trifle

(for six)

8 oz can of pears
6 individual sponge cakes, split in half
strawberry jam
2 oz ratafia biscuits
12 maraschino cherries, chopped
1 tablespoon maraschino syrup
5 tablespoons sherry
3 egg yolks
1 oz caster sugar
1 heaped teaspoon cornflour
½ pint milk
¼ pint double cream
½ oz almonds, blanched, split and
  lightly toasted.

Drain pears, reserving juice, and cut fruit into small pieces. Sandwich sponge cake halves together with jam and arrange with pears on bottom of a shallow, 2 pint serving dish.

Top with ratafia biscuits and sprinkle over chopped cherries, pear juice, maraschino syrup and sherry.

Mix together egg yolks, sugar and cornflour. Warm the milk in a saucepan over low heat until it is hand-hot and pour it on to yolks mixture, stirring constantly. Return mixture to saucepan and cook gently, stirring until it thickens. Do not allow to boil or the custard will curdle. Allow to cool, then pour over the sponge cakes and leave to set before serving.

Whisk the cream until it is thick and spread it over the custard.

Decorate with almonds and more cherries if you like.

Cook's Tip If your custard curdles, tip in a bowl and whisk with a rotary whisk, or if real custard making isn't your forte use canned custard instead. One can is plenty for this trifle.

Caramel Custard

(for four)

Caramel:
3 oz granulated sugar
3 tablespoons water
Custard:
4 eggs
1½ oz caster sugar
few drops of vanilla essence
1 pint milk

To make caramel: put the sugar and water in a heavy saucepan and dissolve sugar over low heat. Bring to the boil and boil until syrup is pale golden brown. Remove from the heat and quickly pour caramel syrup into the bottom of a 1½ pint charlotte mould or cake tin.

For the custard: mix together eggs, sugar and vanilla essence. Warm milk in a saucepan over low heat until it is hand-hot, then pour it onto egg mixture, stirring constantly.

Butter the sides of the mould or tin above the caramel. Strain the custard into the mould or tin and place in a roasting tin half-filled with hot water. Bake in an oven preheated to 300 deg. F., or gas no. 2, for 1½ hours or until a knife inserted into the centre of the custard comes out clean. Do not worry if the custard takes longer to cook than the time given; it will set eventually. Don't increase oven temperature or the custard will have bubbles in.

Remove custard from the oven and leave to cool completely for at least 12 hours or overnight. Turn out carefully on to a flat serving dish.

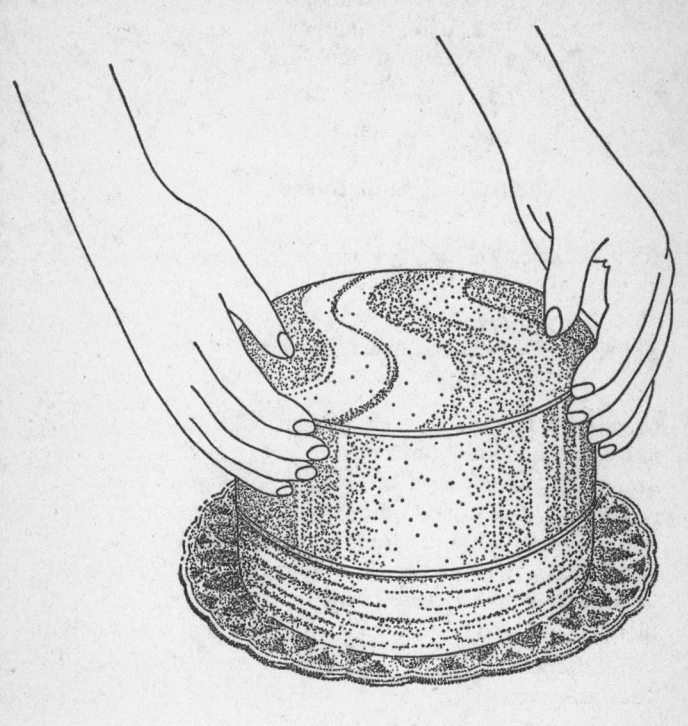

Cook's Tip Never turn out the caramel custard until the moment of serving. The caramel loses its gloss and colour with standing when turned out.

Cherry Cheesecake
(for four to six)

Crust:

5 digestive biscuits, crushed
1 oz butter or margarine
1 oz brown sugar

Cheesecake:

½ packet lemon jelly
3 tablespoons water
8 oz rich cream cheese
5 oz carton plain yogurt
rind and juice large lemon
2 oz caster sugar

Topping:

16 oz can black cherries
1 heaped teaspoon arrowroot

Crush biscuits, add to melted butter and sugar. Line base of 6½ or 7 inch loose-bottomed cake tin. Melt jelly in water in a pan and cool, then add cheese and yogurt mashed together. Add lemon rind, juice and sugar. Pour on to crumbs, set in refrigerator. Before serving, remove tin. Drain cherries saving the juice. Mix about 3 tablespoons of this juice with arrowroot. Boil remainder of juice and pour on blended arrowroot. Return all to pan, boil and allow to thicken. Add cherries. Cool. Pour half cherries in sauce

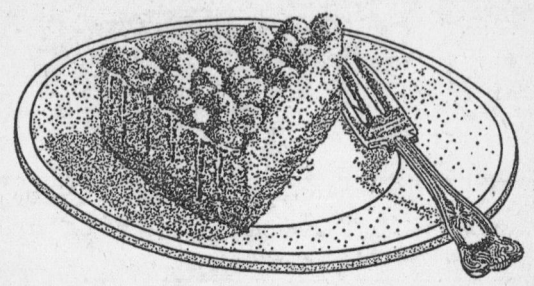

over cheesecake – use remainder to serve later with plain yogurt.

Cook's Tip To crush digestive biscuits without making a mess on the floor, put biscuits into a polythene bag, between a folded teacloth and gently bang with a rolling pin.

HOT.

Cinnamon Apple Pancakes
(makes about eight pancakes)

Batter:

4 oz flour
¼ teaspoon salt
1 egg
½ pint milk
1 tablespoon salad oil
oil for frying

Filling:

4 large Bramley apples, peeled, cored and sliced
¼ teaspoon ground cinnamon
6 oz demerara sugar
6 oz butter

Make the batter in the usual way (see recipe for Lemon Pancakes page 106), and make about 8 pancakes, using a 7 or 8 inch frying pan. Stack pancakes, with a piece of greaseproof paper between each, and set aside.

In a saucepan, gently cook apples, cinnamon, sugar and 4 oz of the butter, stirring occasionally, for about 20 minutes or until apples are tender.

Spread the pancakes out on a flat surface, spoon some of the apple filling on to each and roll them up. In a large frying pan, melt remaining butter. Fry rolled-up pancakes on all sides until they are brown. Pile pancakes on a warm serving dish and sprinkle them with more sugar and cinnamon. Serve hot with cream or ice cream.

Cook's Tip These may be made ahead, then reheated by frying just before serving. Alternatively they may be put in a well buttered roasting tin, brushed with butter and cooked in a very hot oven until brown, about 20 minutes.

Lemon Pancakes
(makes about eight pancakes)

caster sugar
4 oz flour
¼ teaspoon salt
1 egg
½ pint milk
1 tablespoon salad oil
oil for frying
lemon juice

Sprinkle caster sugar on a sheet of greaseproof paper. Set aside.

Sift flour and salt into a mixing bowl and make a well in the centre. Add egg and gradually stir in half the milk. Using a whisk, blend in the flour from sides of the bowl. Beat well until mixture is smooth. Stir in remaining milk and salad oil.

Heat a little oil in a 7 or 8 inch frying pan. When it is hot, pour off any excess oil and spoon about 2 tablespoons of batter into pan. Tip and rotate the pan so that the batter spreads out and thinly covers the bottom of the pan. Cook the pancake for about 1 minute until pale brown underneath. Then turn it over with a palette knife and cook for another minute.

Invert pancake on to sugared greaseproof paper. Sprinkle it with lemon juice and roll it up. Place rolled pancake on a hot serving dish and keep warm while you use remaining batter to make more pancakes in the same way.

Cook's Tip To reheat pancakes, stack on an ovenproof plate and cover with foil. Place in a moderate oven for 30 minutes.

Lemon Meringue Pie
(for six)

Home-made sweet shortcrust pastry:

6 oz plain flour
2 oz butter
2 oz lard
pinch of salt
1 egg yolk
½ oz caster sugar
2 teaspoons water
or
13 oz packet frozen shortcrust pastry, thawed

Lemon filling:

2 large lemons
1½ oz cornflour
½ pint water
2 egg yolks
3 oz caster sugar

Meringue Topping:

3 egg whites
4½ oz caster sugar

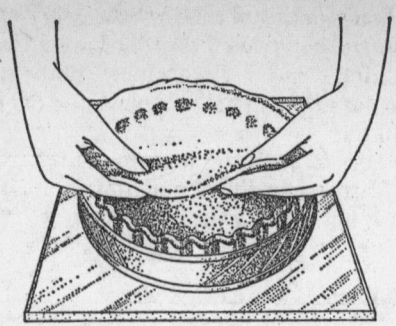

First make pastry. Sift flour and salt into bowl, cut fats into small pieces, then rub into the flour with fingertips until mixture resembles fine breadcrumbs.

Mix egg yolk, sugar and water together. Add this mixture to dry ingredients and bind them together.

Roll out the mixture to a 10 inch circle. Use this to line an 8 inch flan ring or loose-bottomed flan tin placed on a reversed baking tray. Prick base with a fork and chill for ½ hour if time allows. Fill uncooked flan case with a crumpled piece of kitchen foil, or greaseproof paper and baking beans. Bake in preheated oven at 400 deg. F., or gas no. 6, for 15 minutes. Remove foil or greaseproof paper and bake for a further 5 to 10 minutes to dry out the centre. Cool, then remove the flan ring.

Finely grate rind of lemons, squeeze out juice and put in bowl with cornflour. Add 2 tablespoons of water, blend together to form a smooth paste. Boil remaining water and pour it on cornflour mixture. Return mixture to pan, bring it to boiling point and simmer for about 3 minutes until thick, stirring all the time. Remove pan from heat and add egg yolks blended with sugar, return to heat for a moment to allow to thicken. Cool filling slightly and spoon it into flan case. Put to one side.

Whisk egg whites with a rotary whisk until they form stiff peaks. Add sugar, a teaspoon at a time, whisking well after each addition, until all the sugar has been incorporated. Spoon meringue over lemon filling, being careful to cover filling right up to the edge of pastry leaving no air space. Return pie to oven at 325 deg. F., or gas no. 3, for about 30 minutes until pale golden. Serve the pie warm or cold.

Cook's Tip One of the English classics. Not a simple pudding to make but follow these instructions exactly for success. Ideally make and eat on the same day. It is essential to cover the complete flan with meringue leaving no air spaces, otherwise the filling will seep out.

English Custard Tart
(for four to six)

Shortcrust pastry:

4 oz flour
½ teaspoon salt
2 oz butter or margarine
cold water to mix

Custard:

2 eggs
1 oz caster sugar
½ pint milk
grated nutmeg

Sift flour and salt into a bowl. Add butter or margarine and cut into small pieces, then rub fat into flour until the mixture resembles breadcrumbs. Mix in enough water to make a firm dough. Roll out dough and use to line a 7 inch diameter sponge tin or 5 to 6 individual fluted tins about 4½ inch in diameter. Lightly prick base of tin or tins.

To make the custard: beat the eggs and sugar together and stir into the milk. Pour into the pastry case or cases and sprinkle over a little nutmeg. Place the tin or tins on a baking sheet which has been heated in the oven. Put in the oven which has been preheated to 400 deg. F., or gas no. 6. Bake the large flan for 15 minutes then reduce the oven temperature to 350 deg. F., or gas no. 4, and bake for a further 20 to 25 minutes or until the custard filling is set and pale golden brown. The small flans need 10 minutes baking at the hotter temperature, then 15 to 20 minutes after the oven temperature has been reduced. Serve hot or cold.

Cook's Tip As a variation, add 2 oz mixed dried fruit and some freshly grated lemon rind.

Bakewell Tart
(for six)

Pastry:

6 oz plain flour
pinch of salt
1½ oz margarine
1½ oz lard *or* white fat
water to mix

Bakewell filling:

4 level tablespoons raspberry jam
2 oz softened butter
2 oz caster sugar
1 large egg
2 oz self-raising flour
½ level teaspoon baking powder
few drops almond essence

Sieve flour and salt into a bowl. Rub in the fats until mixture resembles fine breadcrumbs, then add sufficient water to mix to a pliable dough. On a floured surface roll out pastry and use to line an 8 inch flan tin or ring on a baking sheet. Trim edges. Spread jam all over the bottom of the pastry.

Place butter, sugar, egg, flour, baking powder and essence in a bowl and beat until thoroughly incorporated, then beat for a further 2 to 3 minutes, preferably with an electric mixer. Spread sponge mixture carefully over the jam and level top. Roll out pastry trimmings and cut 6 strips about ½ inch wide and long enough to go across top of tart. Twist each strip once or twice and lay them loosely over the sponge, three each way to make a lattice. Damp ends and press firmly to edge of pastry. Bake in preheated oven at 375 deg. F., or gas no. 5, for 35 to 40 minutes until sponge is well risen, firm to the touch and golden brown. Serve hot or cold and if liked dredge top of tart lightly with icing sugar.

Cook's Tip Pastry is much easier to roll out if wrapped in foil and chilled for ½ to 1 hour before use. Pastry can be made 1 or 2 days before required and stored in the refrigerator wrapped in foil, polythene or enclosed in an airtight container, but in this case allow it to stand out of the refrigerator for about ½ hour before use, or it will be very hard to roll out.

Sliced Apple Flan

(for four to six)

Pastry:

4 oz plain flour
pinch of salt
1 oz icing sugar
2½ oz butter
water to mix

Apple filling:

2 oz raisins *or* currants
1 oz ground almonds
2 oz demerara sugar
1¼–1½ lb cooking apples
1 level tablespoon salt
4 level tablespoons apricot jam
2 tablespoons water

Sieve flour, salt and icing sugar into a bowl. Add the butter and rub in until mixture resembles fine breadcrumbs. Add sufficient water to mix to a pliable dough. Wrap in polythene or foil and chill for ½ to 1 hour before use. On a floured surface roll out pastry and use to line a 7½ to 8 inch loose-bottomed flan tin.

To make filling: mix raisins, ground almonds and sugar together in a bowl. Peel, quarter and core apples, then thinly slice into a bowl containing ½ pint water and the salt. Rinse apples very well in cold water, drain and arrange a layer of the less even slices in the pastry case. Cover with the raisin mixture, then arrange a neat pattern of remaining apple slices on top. Measure apricot jam into a saucepan and add the water. Bring to the boil, sieve, then brush apples lightly with it. Keep the rest for later. Bake at 400 deg. F., or gas no. 6, for 35 to 40 minutes until pastry is golden brown and the apple tender but not mushy. Reheat jam and spoon over the apples. Serve hot or cold with cream.

Cook's Tip This flan can also be made with sliced apples only and when cooked, be covered with a layer of soured cream and then a layer of demerara sugar. Protect pastry edge with foil, then place under a hot grill until the sugar melts.

home baking

Grantham Gingerbreads

(makes thirty gingerbreads)

4 oz butter
12 oz caster sugar
1 large egg, beaten
9 oz self-raising flour
1–2 level teaspoons ground ginger

Cream the butter until soft, then beat in the sugar until soft and well incorporated. Beat in the egg until thoroughly mixed. Sieve flour and ginger together (if you like a really gingery taste use 2 teaspoons ginger), add to the mixture and work to a firm but pliable dough. Knead lightly then roll the dough into balls about the size of a walnut. Place fairly well apart on well-greased baking sheets. Bake in oven preheated to 300 deg. F., or gas no. 2, for 20 to 30 minutes until well puffed up and lightly browned. Cool on a wire rack.

N.B. Don't be surprised at the first bite, for these biscuits are hollow in the centre.

Cook's Tip Well worth making, they are so delicious. For a variation, these biscuits can be decorated with lemon glacé icing. To 2 teaspoons strained lemon juice beat in sufficient sieved icing sugar to give a fairly stiff icing. Make a greaseproof paper icing bag and fill with icing. Cut off just the very tip of the bag and pipe a lacy pattern over the tops of the biscuits.

Family Flapjacks
(makes thirty-two)

8 oz margarine
8 oz demerara sugar
2 level tablespoons golden syrup
10 oz rolled oats

Grease two 7 inch square shallow tins. Melt margarine in a saucepan, add the sugar and golden syrup and when blended stir in oats. Mix thoroughly. Divide mixture between tins and press down. Bake in the oven preheated to 325 deg. F., gas no. 3, for 25 minutes until just beginning to brown at the edges. Leave to cool for 10 minutes and then mark each into 16 squares, leave in the tin until quite cold. Store in an airtight tin.

Cook's Tip Whilst the oven is on, it is always worth making a couple of tins of these flapjacks, they keep very well. If you haven't two 7 inch square tins, you could put all the mixture into a normal-sized roasting tin about 9 inches square, provided the bottom of the tin is quite flat.

Fruit Malt Loaf

6 oz self-raising flour
1 tablespoon malt drink (Ovaltine)
1 oz caster sugar
3 oz mixed dried fruit
2 level tablespoons (2 oz) golden syrup
⅓ pint milk

Mix all the ingredients to a thick batter, put in a 1 lb loaf tin greased, then bake at 325 deg. F., or gas no. 3, for about 1¼ hours until cooked through in the centre. Serve with butter.

Cook's Tip Very quick to prepare. Weigh all the ingredients straight into the mixing bowl. give it a good stir to blend, then pour it into tin and bake. Best eaten on the day that it is made.

Wheatmeal Bread

Yeast mixture:
¾ pint hand-hot water
1 teaspoon sugar
½ oz dried yeast

Dough:
12 oz strong plain flour
12 oz wholewheat flour
2 teaspoons sugar
2–3 level teaspoons salt
1 tablespoon salad oil

To make yeast mixture: mix water and sugar, stir in dried yeast. Leave for 10 to 15 minutes until frothy.
To make up dough: put all dry ingredients in bowl. Pour on yeast mixture and oil, mix with fork then knead until smooth and no longer sticky – about 10 minutes. Put in a polythene bag greased with ½ teaspoon of vegetable oil and leave to rise in a warm place. Rise until doubled in bulk, this will take about 1 hour at room temperature or leave it to rise overnight in the refrigerator. Knead until back to original bulk, this is called knocking back

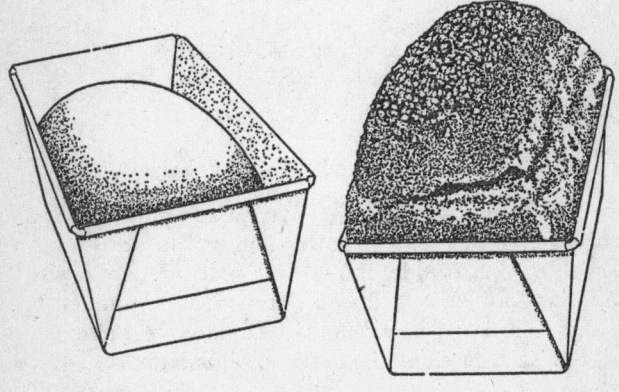

Divide dough into two, mould one half into a round and place in 5 inch well greased and seasoned flower pot. Naturally do not use a plastic flower pot otherwise it would melt in cooking! Shape the second portion of dough and put on a baking sheet or in a greased 1 lb tin. Glaze, sprinkle with cracked wheat. Cover with oiled bag. Put to rise in warm place until double in bulk or the dough has reached top of the tin. Remove bags. Bake in oven at 450 deg. F., or gas no. 8, for 30 to 40 minutes until evenly browned and sounds hollow when tapped on the bottom.

Cook's Tip Dried yeast is excellent for bread making and is available from most chemists and health food stores. It does not keep for ever – 6 months is about the maximum. You will know whether it is fresh when you mix the dried yeast with the hot water and sugar: if the dried yeast is old, it will be inactive and fail to froth, so do not attempt to use it for bread making, go out and buy more. It comes in ½ oz packets, or tins – ½ oz dried yeast equals 1 oz fresh yeast.

Easter Men
(makes three men)

8 oz self-raising flour
½ level teaspoon baking powder
½ teaspoon salt
2 oz Dutch butter
¼ pint milk
3 eggs
milk to glaze
currants, angelica and glacé cherry

Grease a baking sheet. Sieve flour, baking powder and salt into a mixing bowl, add butter and rub in until mixture resembles fine breadcrumbs. Add milk and mix with a knife to form a soft dough. Turn mixture out on to a floured board and knead lightly. Divide into three pieces, roll out each piece of dough to an oblong approx. 6" × 4".

Imagine that the oblong is a clock face and using a knife cut the dough in slits at 2, 4, 6, 8 and 10 o'clock. Pull the dough to form arms and legs and mould the head.

Place men on baking sheet, make a hollow in the middle and put a fresh egg in its shell in the centre, fold arms over the egg. Brush each man with milk to glaze and form the eyes with currants, the nose with angelica and the mouth with a slice of glacé cherry. Place in centre of the oven preheated to 400 deg. F., or gas no. 6, for about 13 to 15 minutes. Gently ease egg out and place in an egg cup, eat with the Easter men.

Cook's Tip An idea from Holland. Serve Easter men for Easter Sunday morning. Older children no doubt will help to make them. Inexpensive to make from the basic scone dough. Handle as little as possible for a light result. If you are making hot cross buns for Easter, use some of the dough for making Easter Men. Use 5 oz of made dough for each man.

Fresh Lemon Fingers
(makes twenty-four fingers)

6 oz self-raising flour
6 oz softened butter
6 oz caster sugar
2 eggs
juice and rind of 1 lemon
4 oz granulated sugar

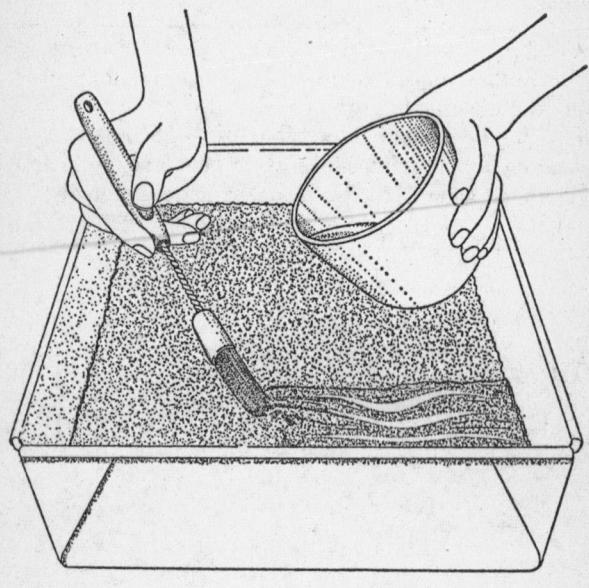

Grease an 8″ × 12″ swiss roll tin and line the base with greased greaseproof paper. Put the flour, butter, caster sugar, eggs and grated rind in a bowl and blend together with a fork until smooth. Spread in the tin and bake in the centre of the preheated oven at 350 deg. F., or gas no. 4, for 15 to 20 minutes until well risen and golden brown. While sponge is baking, make a paste of lemon juice and granulated sugar. When the sponge comes out of the oven spread lemon sugar paste over the top while it is still hot. Leave in tin to cool and crisp the top. Cut into 3 long strips then each strip into 8 fingers, making 24 fingers in all.

Cook's Tip Make sure that the butter is really soft before mixing all the ingredients together, otherwise the result will not be even. Never waste lemon rind if only using lemon juice in a recipe. First finely grate off the rind, mix it with caster sugar and keep in a screw topped jar and use for cakes and Victoria sandwiches.

Simnel Cake

6 oz butter, softened
6 oz soft brown sugar
3 eggs
6 oz plain flour
3 level teaspoons mixed spice and
1 level teaspoon baking powder,
   sieved together
2 tablespoons milk
10 oz mixed dried fruit
2 oz glacé cherries, chopped
1 oz mixed cut peel, chopped
grated rind of 1 lemon
2 oz ground almonds

Decoration:

1 lb almond paste
1 tablespoon sieved apricot jam
1 egg white
4–6 oz icing sugar, sieved
foil-wrapped chocolate Easter eggs
bow of ribbon

Grease 7 inch round cake tin and line with greased greaseproof paper. Put all cake ingredients together in a mixing bowl and beat together with a wooden spoon until well mixed (2 to 3 minutes). Place half mixture in cake tin. Smooth top. Roll one-third of almond paste to a 7 inch round and place on top of cake mixture. Put remaining cake mixture in tin and smooth top. Bake in preheated oven at 300 deg. F., or gas no. 2, for $2\frac{1}{2}$ hours. Cool on a wire rack.

Brush top of cake with boiled, sieved apricot jam. Roll out one-third of remaining almond paste to a 7 inch round and place on cake, pinch edges. Roll out remaining almond paste into 11 balls and arrange around the edge of cake. If liked, brush with a little beaten egg and bake at 425 deg. F., or gas no. 7 for 2 to 3 minutes to brown the almond paste lightly. Cool, mix remaining egg white with icing sugar and pour into centre of cake. When set, decorate with Easter eggs and chickens.

Cook's Tip An easy cake made by the all-in-the-bowl-together method. It is essential that the butter is very soft but not oily. If you don't want to decorate the cake and just want the almond filling, make half the amount of almond paste.

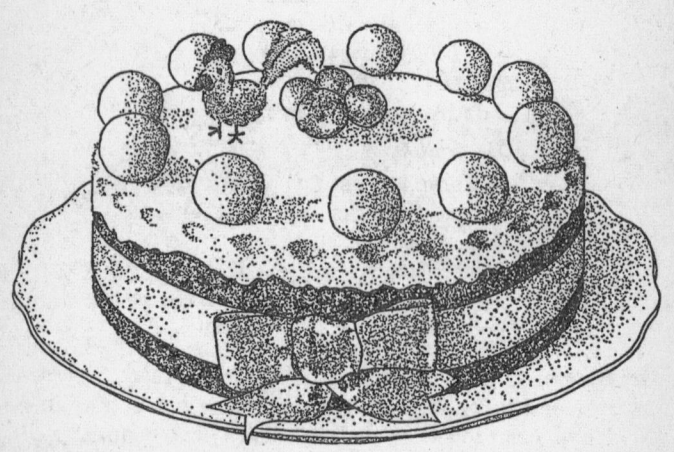

Mixed Fruit and Pineapple Cake

2 oz glacé cherries
7 oz self-raising flour
1 lb can of pineapple chunks, rings *or* crushed, excluding the juice
5 oz butter
4½ oz soft brown sugar
2 large eggs, blended
2 tablespoons milk
12 oz mixed dried fruit

Grease an 8 inch round cake tin and line with greased greaseproof paper. Cut cherries into halves. Roll the halved cherries in flour. Drain and chop pineapple very finely. Cream butter and sugar together until light and creamy.

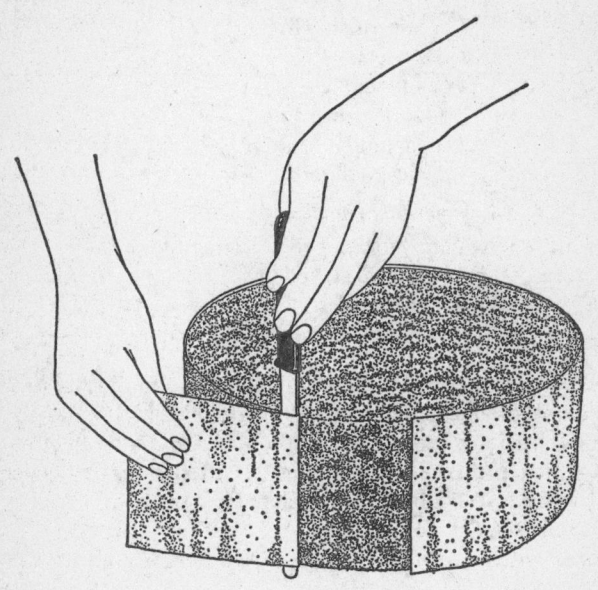

Beat in eggs, adding a tablespoon of flour with the last amount of egg. Fold in flour, milk and last of all the fruit, including pineapple. Turn into the prepared tin, place in the centre of the oven preheated to 325 deg. F., or gas no. 3, and bake for about 2 hours until pale golden, shrinking slightly away from the sides of the tin. Leave to cool in tin, remove paper and store in plastic container in the refrigerator as this is a very moist cake.

Cook's Tip Because canned pineapple is added to this fruit cake, it needs special care in storage. Keep it wrapped or in a container in the refrigerator for up to 2 months. It is beautifully moist and a really special cake. A larger version could be used as a lighter coloured Christmas fruit cake.

Chocolate Brownies
(makes about sixteen)

4 oz self-raising flour
$1\frac{1}{2}$ oz cocoa
4 oz butter
5 oz soft brown sugar
2 eggs, lightly beaten
1 tablespoon milk

Chocolate Fudge Icing:

$1\frac{1}{2}$ oz butter
1 oz cocoa, sieved
about 3 tablespoons milk
4 oz icing sugar, sieved

Sieve flour and cocoa into a mixing bowl. In another bowl, cream together butter and brown sugar with a wooden spoon until mixture is light and fluffy. Gradually beat eggs into butter mixture, then fold in sifted flour and cocoa with the milk. Mix well till smooth. Spoon into a lined, greased $7'' \times 7'' \times 1\frac{1}{2}''$ deep tin.

Bake in the oven preheated to 375 deg. F., or gas no. 5,

for 30 minutes or until centre of the cake springs back when lightly pressed with a fingertip. Turn cake out on to a wire rack and cool.

To make icing: melt butter in a small pan. Stir in cocoa and cook very gently for 1 minute. Remove pan from the heat and stir in milk and icing sugar. Mix well to a spreading consistency. Spread icing over the cake and leave to set. Cut into squares.

Cook's Tip American brownies are very, very sweet. This is an anglicised version with less sugar than they would use. Cocoa must always be sieved for recipes as it is inclined to be lumpy.

Express Chocolate Cake

(for six to eight)

6½ oz plain flour
2 tablespoons cocoa
1 level teaspoon bicarbonate of soda
1 level teaspoon baking powder
5 oz caster sugar
2 tablespoons golden syrup
2 eggs lightly beaten
¼ pint salad *or* corn oil
¼ pint milk

Filling and Icing:
¼ pint whipping cream
apricot jam
3 oz plain chocolate
grated chocolate *or* chocolate curls

Sieve flour, cocoa, bicarbonate of soda and baking powder into a large mixing bowl. Make a well in centre and add sugar and syrup. Gradually stir in the eggs, oil and milk and beat well to make a smooth batter.

Pour batter into two greased and lined 8 inch sandwich tins.

Bake in the oven preheated to 325 deg. F., or gas no. 3, for 30 to 35 minutes, or until cakes spring back when lightly pressed with a fingertip. Turn cakes out on to a wire rack and leave to cool.

Whip cream until it will stand in soft peaks. Sandwich the cakes together with cream and apricot jam. Melt chocolate gently on a plate over a pan of hot water, do not stir or it will harden. Spread it over top of the cake. Decorate the edge with grated plain or milk chocolate or curls.

Cook's Tip This recipe keeps extra well if iced with the chocolate fudge icing used for the Chocolate Brownies on page 126.

Chocolate Rum Truffles
(makes about four dozen truffles)

2 oz seedless raisins, chopped
2 oz glacé cherries, chopped
4 tablespoons rum
8 oz sweet biscuits, crushed
8 oz stale cake, crumbled
5 tablespoons drinking chocolate
2 tablespoons apricot jam, melted
3 oz chocolate vermicelli

Put raisins and cherries in a small bowl with rum and leave to soak for 2 hours.

Mix together crushed biscuits and cake crumbs in a large mixing bowl. Add drinking chocolate and soaked raisins and cherries and mix well, pounding with the back of a wooden spoon. Alternatively, use an electric mixer with a dough hook or the beater on slow speed.

Stir in the melted jam, adding more if necessary to make a firm sticky dough. Shape the dough into small balls, put them into a polythene bag with the chocolate vermicelli, coat them by shaking the bag. Leave truffles on a tray or flat plates overnight to become firm, then place them in sweet cases.

Cook's Tip If you would like very potent rum-flavoured truffles, add more rum to the dough and leave it in the refrigerator overnight before rolling into balls.

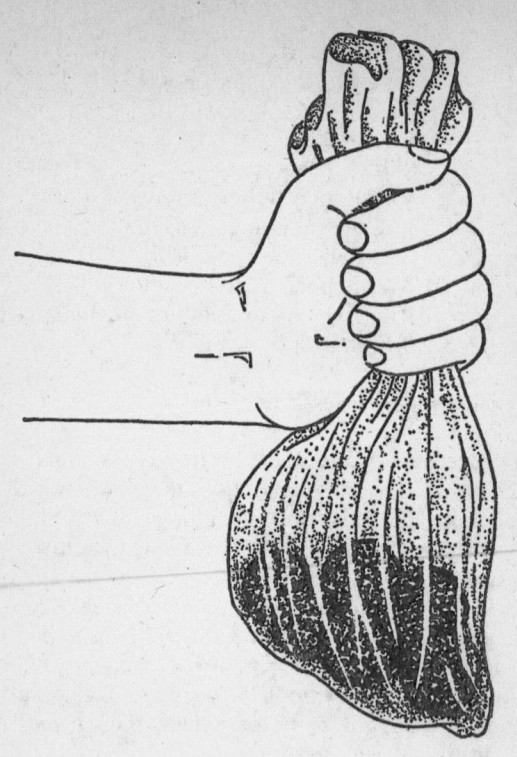

preserves for the larder shelf

Concentrated Mint Sauce

¼ pint malt vinegar
4 oz granulated sugar
1 pint measure finely chopped mint

Pick the mint when it is young and plentiful.

Put vinegar and sugar in a pan, bring to boil, stirring until sugar has dissolved, boil for 1 minute.

Stir in mint, remove from heat and turn into a 1 lb screw topped jar. Leave to cool, label and store on the larder shelf. To use, put required amount in a sauceboat, thin down with little vinegar and sugar to taste if liked.

Cook's Tip Making a concentrate like this means that you have mint sauce throughout the winter. Store in a cool larder until the season comes round again.

Miranda's Rhubarb and Apple Chutney
(makes about 8 lbs)

3 lb apples
1½ pints malt vinegar
1 lb rhubarb
2 lb soft brown sugar
8 oz chopped dates
8 oz sultanas
1 small red pepper
1 tablespoon ginger powder
2 tablespoons pickling spice, ground
1 teaspoon mixed spice
1 dessertspoon cumin seed
1 teaspoon cayenne pepper
2 tablespoons salt

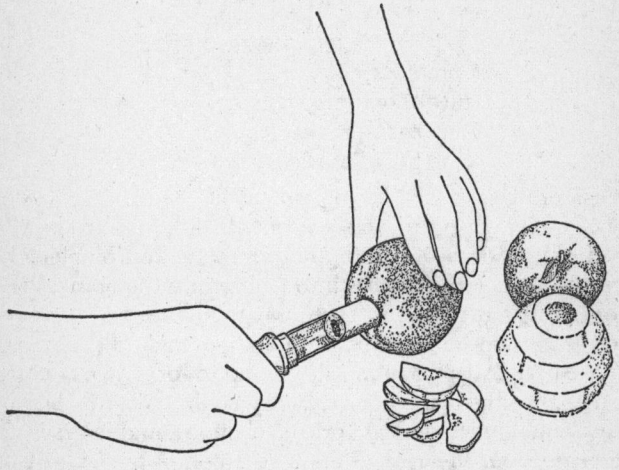

Peel, core and roughly chop the apples and place in a pan with half the vinegar and cook to a pulp. Slice the rhubarb into small pieces and place in a large pan with the remaining vinegar and bring to the boil; simmer for 5 minutes then add to the apple purée, sugar, dates and sultanas. Seed and chop the pepper and add to the pan with the spices and salt. Bring to the boil and simmer gently for 15 to 20 minutes or until fairly thick and clear looking. Pour into jars and cover. Store for 2 to 3 months before using.

Cook's Tip   This is a good way of using up the last of the rhubarb and windfall apples at the end of the season and makes a very reasonably-priced chutney if the rhubarb and windfall apples are free. It is essential to use a covering to the jars that is moisture proof. Clean honey screw-topped jars are ideal, or use plastic snap-on lids or seal with melted paraffin wax.

Seville Orange And Apricot Marmalade
(makes about 4½ lbs)

1¼ lb Seville oranges
2 pints water
juice of one large lemon
15 oz can apricots
2½ lb granulated sugar

Wash oranges, put in large pan – about 7 pint size – cover with water. Bring to boil, cover with lid. Simmer gently until skin of oranges is soft, about 2 hours. Test by piercing with a pin head; if it goes into fruit easily the oranges are done. Lift out fruit, cut each orange in half, remove pips and put them to one side. Slice oranges and add to liquid in the pan. Put pips in muslin, tie up to form bag. Reduce contents of the pan by one third by boiling with the lid off. Add lemon juice, canned apricots chopped, and juices from the can. Pour in sugar, bring to the boil over low heat to dissolve the sugar, then boil rapidly until setting point, about 15 minutes. Pour into hot, clean, dry jars. Cover and label in usual way.

Cook's Tip The re-usable plastic lids used for covering the 1 lb jars can be obtained from: A. W. Gregory & Co Ltd, Glynde House, Glynde Street, London, S.E.4. To use frozen Seville oranges for marmalade take this method, i.e. the whole fruit method, and do not thaw before making the marmalade, otherwise the colour will be poor. Add an extra orange per 5 lb fruit if using frozen oranges to give a good set.

Minced Peel Marmalade
(*yield* 10 *lbs*)

3 lb bitter Seville oranges
2 lemons
5 pints water
6 lb granulated sugar

Wash fruit, then cut in half and squeeze out juice and put juice in a large bowl. Cut fruit skin into quarters, put pips in a piece of muslin and tie with string to form bag. Using a coarse blade, mince peel into large bowl containing juice.

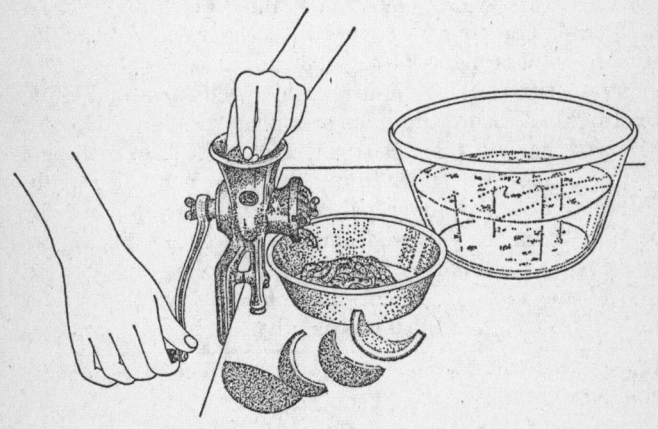

Transfer to preserving or large pan. Put in muslin bag and tie end of string to pan handle. Add water and bring slowly to the boil. Simmer gently for two hours with lid off until peel is tender and contents of pan have reduced by half. Add sugar. Stir over low heat until sugar has dissolved, bring up to the boil and cook rapidly until setting point is reached (about 20 minutes, 220 deg. F.).

Draw pan off heat, cool for 10 to 15 minutes, then pour into hot, clean, dry jars. Cover and label in usual way.

Cook's Tip It is essential in marmalade making to ensure that the peel is really tender before adding the sugar. If peel is boiled with sugar for considerably more than 25 minutes it becomes tough.

Apple and Blackberry Jelly
(makes about 3 lb)

4 lb cooking apples
2 lb blackberries
2 pints water
sugar

Wash and cut up the apples, removing any bad portions. Wash the blackberries and drain, place in a large pan with the apples and water, cover and simmer until the fruit is a soft pulp. The time will vary with the variety of apples used but will probably be about 30 minutes.

Strain the fruit through a scalded jelly bag and leave overnight. Measure the juice and place in a large pan and bring to the boil. Add the sugar, allowing 1 lb to each pint of juice. Allow the sugar to dissolve and then boil rapidly for 10 minutes. Remove pan from the heat and test for setting. Skim the jelly and pour at once into warmed jars and cover with waxed circles. Leave to cool.

Seal and store in a cool dark place away from strong light. This will give 5 to 6 jars of jelly.

Cook's Tip To test for setting take a scant teaspoon of the jelly and put in a cold saucer. After a few minutes the surface should begin to set and crinkle when pushed with a finger. Do not boil the jelly rapidly while the test is going on, otherwise setting points may be lost. A very good home-made concentrated drink can be made by boiling up the fruit pulp from the bag with 3 pints of water and 12 oz sugar. Strain and pour into bottles. Keep in the refrigerator and dilute to taste with water and ice cubes.

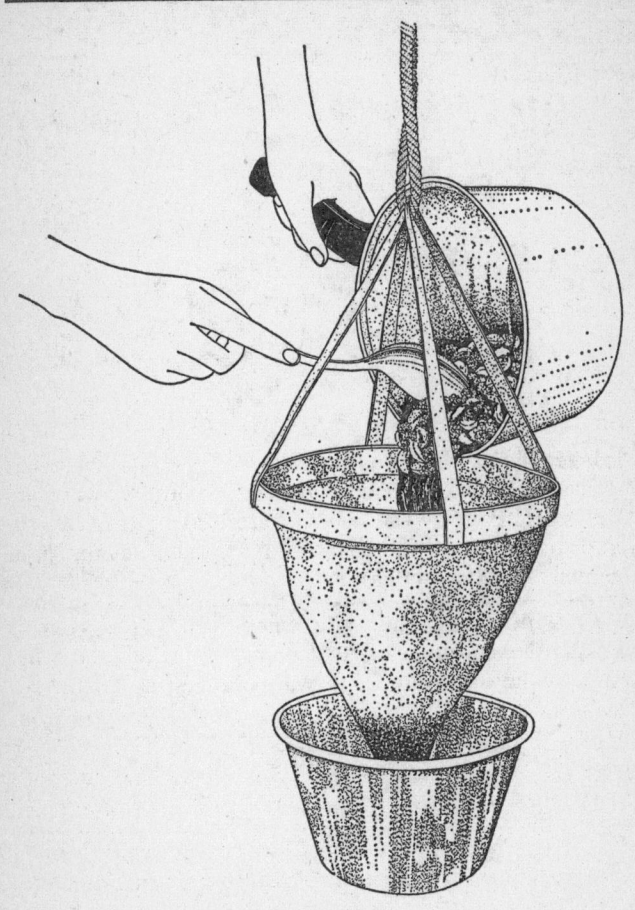

Fresh Lemon Drink

3 large lemons
4 oz caster sugar

1¾ pints boiling water
12 ice cubes
} *or* 2 pints water and keep in refrigerator

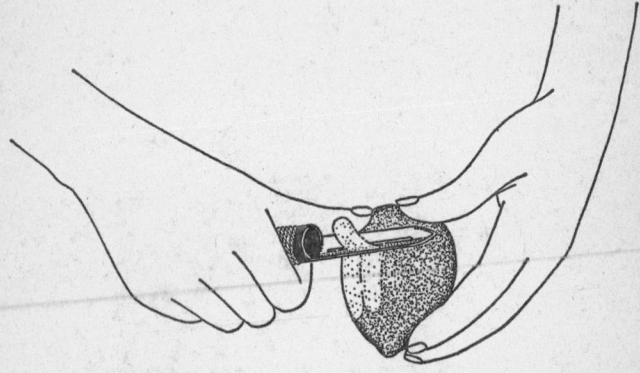

Peel lemons as thinly as possible using a potato peeler. Squeeze juice from lemons. Put peel in a large bowl or jug with sugar. Pour on the boiling water. Cover and leave to stand overnight. Next day add reserved lemon juice strained. Add 12 ice cubes.

Cook's Tip This home-made lemon drink is really fruity and has the sharpness of the lemon peel included. Do not try to make a similar drink with oranges as it will lack flavour.

christmas comes every year

(All recipes are for six)

Roast Stuffed Turkey

12 lb dressed turkey
2 oz butter
6 streaky bacon rashers, rinds removed

Chestnut Stuffing:

8 oz can unsweetened chestnut purée *or*
1 lb chestnuts
4 oz fresh brown breadcrumbs
grated rind of $\frac{1}{2}$ lemon
1 large egg, beaten
2 oz butter, melted
salt and pepper

Lemon and sausage stuffing:

turkey liver, finely chopped
1 oz butter
12 oz pork sausagemeat
1 onion, finely chopped
8 oz fresh white breadcrumbs
2–3 tablespoons chopped parsley
1 teaspoon dried thyme
grated rind and juice of 1 lemon
1 teaspoon salt
$\frac{1}{8}$ teaspoon black pepper
1 egg, beaten

Wipe inside and outside of turkey with a clean damp cloth. Set aside.

If you are using fresh chestnuts, make a slit in each one with a sharp knife and cook in boiling water for 5 minutes. Drain and cool slightly. Remove skins and return chestnuts to pan with just enough stock or water to cover. Simmer for about 20 minutes or until chestnuts are tender. Drain thoroughly and push chestnuts through a sieve or purée in a blender.

To make chestnut stuffing: combine all ingredients well, seasoning liberally with salt and pepper. Set aside.

To make lemon and sausage stuffing: fry liver in butter for 5 minutes, stirring frequently. Add all remaining ingredients and mix thoroughly. Set aside.

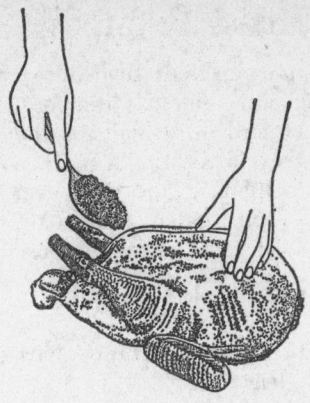

Stuff the tail end of the turkey with chestnut mixture. Stuff the neck end with lemon and sausage mixture. Fold over the flap and secure with a skewer. Truss turkey with string or skewers and place it in a roasting tin. Spread bird with butter and place bacon rashers over the breast. Cover loosely with foil and place in the oven preheated to 350 deg. F., or gas no. 4. Roast for 15 minutes per lb plus 15 minutes over. Remove foil for the last 30 to 40 minutes and baste occasionally. The turkey is cooked when the meat is pierced with a skewer and the juice that runs out is clear.

Transfer turkey to a serving plate and remove skewers and string. Garnish with parsley or watercress, bacon rolls and grilled sausages and serve.

Bacon Rolls

Remove rinds from 6 streaky bacon rashers. Stretch rashers on a wooden board with the back of a knife until they are almost twice their original length. Cut each rasher in 2 and roll up each piece. Secure rolls with thin skewers and grill for about 5 minutes, turning once or until they are golden brown.

Roast Potatoes

Peel 2 lb potatoes and cut them into even-sized pieces. Cook them in boiling salted water for 5 minutes. Meanwhile, melt 3 oz lard in a small roasting tin in the oven (where the turkey is roasting). Drain potatoes well and transfer them to the tin. Turn them over in the hot fat so that they are evenly coated. Return tin to the oven and roast potatoes for 1 hour or until they are tender.

Glazed Carrots

$1\frac{1}{2}$ lb carrots, cut into quarters
    lengthwise
$1\frac{1}{2}$ oz butter
salt
1 teaspoon caster sugar
grated nutmeg
1 tablespoon chopped parsley

Put carrots in a saucepan with $\frac{1}{2}$ oz of butter, salt, sugar and just enough water to cover. Cover pan and simmer for about 15 minutes or until carrots are tender. Remove lid and continue to simmer until almost all the liquid has evaporated, and transfer them to a serving dish. Sprinkle with nutmeg, dot with remaining butter cut into small pieces, and scatter with chopped parsley.

Bread Sauce

2 cloves
1 onion
$\frac{1}{2}$ pint milk
2 oz fresh white breadcrumbs
salt and pepper
$\frac{1}{2}$ oz butter

Stick cloves into the onion and put it in a saucepan with milk. Heat gently to boiling point, then turn off the heat and leave milk to infuse for 30 minutes.

Remove onion and cloves from pan and stir in breadcrumbs, seasoning and butter. Reheat sauce almost to boiling point, then remove it from the heat. Cover with a piece of greaseproof paper dampened with water and keep warm.

Rich Gravy

> turkey giblets
> 2 onions, halved
> 1 bayleaf
> 1 parsley sprig
> 1 mace blade
> 1½ pints water
> 2 tablespoons turkey fat
> 1 oz flour
> salt and pepper
> 3 tablespoons sherry
> gravy browning

Put giblets in a saucepan with onions, bayleaf, parsley sprig, mace blade and water. Cover pan tightly and bring to the boil. Simmer for about 3 hours. Strain giblet stock and set aside.

In another saucepan, blend together turkey fat and flour. Cook over low heat stirring constantly, until the roux (fat and flour mixture) turns brown. Gradually add giblet stock, stirring constantly. Bring to the boil and simmer for 2 minutes, stirring, or until gravy has thickened slightly. Add seasoning to taste, sherry and a few drops of gravy browning if necessary to make gravy rich brown in colour.

Mince Pie

8 oz flour
½ teaspoon salt
6 oz lard, chilled and cut into ½ inch cubes
about ¼ pint cold water
1 lb jar mincemeat
milk
caster sugar

Sift flour and salt into a mixing bowl. Add cubes of lard and just enough water to make firm pastry, mixing with a sharp knife. On a lightly floured surface, roll out pastry to a strip about ½ inch thick and 6 inches wide. Fold pastry in 3 and give it a quarter turn to the left. Roll out again into a strip and fold in 3. Wrap pastry in greaseproof paper and chill in refrigerator for 30 minutes.

Divide pastry into 2 portions, one slightly larger than the other. Roll out smaller portion to a ¼ inch thick circle and use it to line an 8 inch pie dish (preferably made of enamel or tin). Spoon mincemeat into the dish.

Roll out remaining pastry to a circle about ¼ inch thick. Brush edges of pastry already in the tin with milk and cover mincemeat filling with the second pastry circle. Press edges together to seal, trim off excess pastry and crimp edges to make a decorative finish. Place in the refrigerator to chill for 10 minutes.

Brush top of pie with milk and place it in the oven preheated to 425 deg. F., or gas no. 7. Bake for 25 minutes or until the pastry is golden brown. Sprinkle with caster sugar immediately. Serve warm.

Brandy Butter

3 oz unsalted butter
6 oz icing sugar, sifted
2–3 tablespoons brandy

Cream butter with a wooden spoon until it is soft. Gradually beat in icing sugar and continue beating until mixture is light and fluffy. Beat in brandy.

Turn brandy butter into a serving dish and chill in refrigerator to harden before using. Remove butter from the refrigerator 30 minutes before serving.

Rum Sauce

1 oz butter
1 oz flour
½ pint milk
1 oz caster sugar
3–4 tablespoons rum

Melt butter in a small saucepan. Remove pan from heat and stir in flour. Return pan to heat and cook roux gently for 1 minute (don't let it turn brown). Gradually add milk, stirring constantly. Stir in sugar and bring to the boil. Simmer sauce for 2 to 3 minutes, stirring until it has thickened. Stir in rum.

Remove pan from the heat. Cover with a piece of buttered damp greaseproof paper and keep warm.

INDEX

Apple Baked Collar, 46
   and Blackberry Jelly, 136
Apricot and Lemon Flan, 99
   Yogurt Fool, 98

BACON
Apple Baked Collar, 46
Golden Nuggets, 47
Bacon Rolls, 141

Baked Onions, 85
Bakewell Tart, 111
Barbados Cream, 94
Basic Savoury Mince, 30

BEEF
Beefburgers, Home-made, 31
Brisket, Pot Roast, 29
   Slow Roasted, 23
Carbonnade of, 25
Casserole, Bristol Beef, 20
   Summer, 23
Chilli Con Carne, 31
Cottage Pie, 31
Family Meat Loaf, 21
Goulash, 24

Mince, Basic Savoury, 30
    Bolognaise or tomato, 31
    Cabbage Leaves, Stuffed, 31
    Cottage Pie, 30
Pressed, 27
Slade's Pie, 22
Stew with Herb Dumplings, 26

Beetroot Soup, 10
Bolognaise Mince, 31
Boned Shoulder of Lamb with Savoury Green Stuffing, 32
Brandy Butter, 145
Bread Sauce, 142
Bristol Beef Casserole, 20

CAKES & BISCUITS
Chocolate Brownies, 126
    Cake, Express, 128
    Rum Truffles, 129
Easter Men, 120
Family Flapjacks, 117
Fresh Lemon Fingers, 122
Fruit Malt Loaf, 118
Grantham Gingerbreads, 116
Mixed Fruit and Pineapple Cake, 125
Simnel Cake, 123

Caramel Custard, 102
Carbonnade of Beef, 25
Cherry Cheesecake, 104
Chestnut Stuffing, 140

CHICKEN
    with Cider and Mushroom Sauce, 60
    Country Chicken Pie, 57
    Herby Chicken and Ham Pie, 62
    in Lemon Mayonnaise, 54
    and Liver Terrine, 64

    in Orange Cream Sauce, 55
    Poule Au Pot Au Citron, 61
    Savoury Stuffed Pancakes, 65
    Sicilian Chicken, 59

Chilli Con Carne, 31
Cinnamon Apple Pancakes, 105
Chocolate Brownies, 126
    Rum Truffles, 129

Coleslaw Salad, 76
Concentrated Mint Sauce, 132
Cottage Pie, 31
Country Chicken Pie, 57
Crunchy Pork and Cabbage, 45
Curried Egg Mayonnaise, 77

EGGS
Easter Men, 120
Easy Tomato Soup, 11

Omelettes: Cheese, 70
    Fine Herbs, 70
    Ham, 70
    Mushroom, 70
    Spanish, 70
    Tomato, 70
Soft-Boiled Eggs in Onion Sauce, 67
Supper Baked Eggs, 68

English Custard Tart, 109
Express Chocolate Cake, 128

Family Flapjacks, 117
    Meat Loaf, 21

FISH
Kipper Scramble, 73

Jugged Kippers, 72
Tuna Spaghetti Bake, 73

French Dressing, 79
Fresh Lemon Drink, 138
   Fingers, 122
Fruit Malt Loaf, 118

Garlic Rolls, 68
Ginger and Sherry Dessert, 92
Glazed Carrots, 142
Gooseberry Fool, 91
Grantham Gingerbreads, 116

Helen's Chocolate Cream Layer Pudding, 94
Herby Chicken and Ham Pie, 62
Home-made Beefburgers, 31
   Yogurt, 99

KIPPERS
Jugged Kippers, 72
Kipper Pâté, 16
   Scramble, 73

LAMB
Boned Shoulder of Lamb with Savoury Green Stuffing, 32
Irish Stew, 35
Red Hot Lamb, 36
Stuffed Apricot Lamb, 33

Leek and Tomato Flan, 84
Lemon Meringue Pie, 107
Lemon Pancakes, 106
   and Sausage Stuffing, 140
Liver Kebabs, 38

Mayonnaise, 77

MEAT

Beef: Beefburgers, Home-made, 31
  Brisket, Pot Roast, 29
    Slow Roasted, 23
  Carbonnade of Beef, 25
  Casserole, Bristol, 20
    Summer, 23
  Chilli Con Carne, 31
  Cottage Pie, 30
  Family Meat Loaf, 21
  Goulash, 24
  Mince: Basic Savoury, 30
    Bolognaise or Tomato, 31
    Cabbage Leaves, Stuffed, 31
    Cottage Pie, 30
  Pressed, 27
  Slade's Pie, 22
  Stew with Herb Dumplings, 26

Bacon: Apple Baked Collar, 46
  Golden Nuggets, 47
  Rolls, 141

Chicken: with Cider and Mushroom Sauce, 60
  Country Chicken Pie, 57
  Herby Chicken and Ham Pie, 62
  in Lemon Mayonnaise, 54
  and Liver Terrine, 64
  in Orange Cream Sauce, 55
  Poule Au Pot Au Citron, 61
  Savoury Stuffed Pancakes, 65
  Sicilian Chicken, 59

Lamb: Boned Shoulder with Savoury Green Stuffing, 32
  Irish Stew, 35
  Red Hot Lamb, 36
  Stuffed Apricot Lamb, 33
Liver Kebabs, 38

Pork: Chops in Barbecue Sauce, 42
    with Cider and Mushroom Sauce, 41
  Crunchy Pork and Cabbage, 45
  Pork with Spiced Mushroom Cream Sauce, 40
  Sausagemeat: Sausageburger Toad in the Hole, 49
    Hunter's Roll, 50
  Spicy Pork Balls, 43

Turkey: Roast Stuffed Turkey, 140
  Spring Turkey Mayonnaise, 52

Meringues, 96
Midsummer Pudding, 90
Minced Peel Marmalade, 135
Mince Pie, 144
Minestrone Chicken Soup, 12
Miranda's Rhubarb and Apple Chutney, 133
Mixed Fruit and Pineapple Cake, 125

Pâté, Kipper, 16
Potato and Onion Bake, 87

PORK
Crunchy Pork and Cabbage, 45
Pork Chops in Barbecue Sauce, 42
  with Cider and Mushroom Sauce, 41
Pork with Spiced Mushroom Cream Sauce, 40
Sausagemeat: Sausageburger Toad in the Hole, 49
  Hunter's Roll, 50
Spicy Pork Balls, 43

Pot Roast Brisket, 29
Poule Au Pot Au Citron, 61

PRESERVES
Apple and Blackberry Jelly, 136
Concentrated Mint Sauce, 132
Fresh Lemon Drink, 138
Minced Peel Marmalade, 135

Miranda's Rhubarb and Apple Chutney, 133
Seville Orange and Apricot Marmalade, 134

Pressed Beef, 27

PUDDINGS & SWEETS
Apricot and Lemon Flan, 99
   Yogurt Fool, 98
Bakewell Tart, 111
Barbados Cream, 94
Brandy Butter, 145
Caramel Custard, 102
Cherry Cheesecake, 104
Cinnamon Apple Pancakes, 105
English Custard Tart, 109
Ginger and Sherry Dessert, 92
Gooseberry Fool, 91
Helen's Chocolate Cream Layer Pudding, 93
Home-made Yogurt, 99
Lemon Meringue Pie, 107
   Pancakes, 106
Meringues, 96
Midsummer Pudding, 90
Mince Pie, 144
Old Fashioned Trifle, 101
Raspberry Meringue Basket, 97
Rum Sauce, 145
Sliced Apple Flan, 113
Suety Pudding, 37
Syllabub, 95

Red Cabbage, 86
Rich Gravy, 143
   Onion Soup, 13
Roast Potatoes, 142
   Stuffed Turkey, 140
Rosti, 88
Rum Sauce, 145

SALADS & VEGETABLES
Cabbage, Red, 86
Carrots, Glazed, 142
Coleslaw Salad, 76
Egg Mayonnaise, Curried, 77
Leek and Tomato Flan, 84
Marrow, Stuffed, 82
Onions, Baked, 85
Peppers, Red, with Cheese Sauce, 80
Potato and Onion Bake, 87
Potatoes, Roast, 142
Rosti, 88
Tomatoes, Stuffed, 81
Vegetables, Summer au Gratin, 83

Sausageburger Toad in the Hole, 49
Savoury Stuffed Pancakes, 65
Scottish Vegetable Soup, 14
Seville Orange and Apricot Marmalade, 134
Sicilian Chicken, 59
Simnel Cake, 123
Slade's Pie, 22
Slow Roasted Brisket, 23
Soft-Boiled Eggs in Onion Sauce, 67

SOUPS
Beetroot, 10
Easy Tomato, 11
Minestrone Chicken, 12
Rich Onion, 13
Scottish Vegetable, 14
Spinach, 15

Sliced Apple Flan, 113
Spicy Pork Balls, 43
Spinach Soup, 15
Spring Turkey Mayonnaise, 52
Stocks, 10

Stuffed Apricot Lamb, 33
    Cabbage Leaves, 31
    Marrow, 82
    Red Peppers with Cheese Sauce, 80
    Tomatoes, 81
Stuffing: Chestnut, 140
    Lemon and Sausage, 140
Suety Pudding, 37
Summer Casserole, 23
    Vegetables au Gratin, 83
Supper Baked Eggs, 68
Syllabub, 95

Toast Hawaii, 53
Tuna Spaghetti Bake, 73

TURKEY
Roast Stuffed Turkey, 140
Spring Turkey Mayonnaise, 52

Wheatmeal Bread, 119

GROWING, FREEZING & COOKING

Keith Mossman and Mary Norwak

Growing, Freezing & Cooking provides a complete reference book for all who want the best results from their garden produce. It provides information on basic methods of gardening and freezing, and an alphabetical guide to many vegetables, herbs and fruits; under each heading will be found advice on cultivation and choice of varieties, followed by freezing recommendations, and recipes for each product.

For all those households where gardening and cooking are regular activities, and for the ever-burgeoning ranks of freezer-owners, this book by two experts will prove invaluable.

60p

HOME FREEZING - A BEGINNER'S GUIDE

Mary Norwak

This is the first simple guide to food freezing which answers your questions without assuming you know half the answers before you start.

At a glance, the short notes and clear diagrams will tell you how to deal with fresh raw materials, cooked dishes and bulk purchases of frozen food. The book presents a step-by-step guide for the complete beginner, and a quick reference guide for the more experienced freezer-owner.

There are notes on choosing and installing a freezer, what to put in it, how to choose and use packaging and how to avoid costly mistakes. All this essential information, presented in the simplest way, will ensure that every beginner to home freezing soon becomes an expert.

60p

CALENDAR OF HOME FREEZING

Mary Norwak

In this month-by-month guide to successful home freezing Mary Norwak helps you to use your freezer to the best advantage, and to make the most of seasonal produce. The leading expert on home freezing, she provides invaluable advice on bulk buying for home freezing, seasonal buying and preservation, prepare-ahead meals and menus and recipes for home freezing.

Calendar of Home Freezing is an excellent handbook for use the whole year through – no freezer-owning household should be without it!

60p

All Sphere Books are available at your bookshop or newsagent, or can be ordered from the following address:
Sphere Books, Cash Sales Department,
P.O. Box 11, Falmouth, Cornwall.

Please send cheque or postal order (no currency), and allow 18p for postage and packing for the first book plus 8p per copy for each additional book ordered up to a maximum charge of 66p in U.K.

Customers in Eire and B.F.P.O. please allow 18p for postage and packing for the first book plus 8p per copy for the next 6 books, thereafter 3p per book.

Overseas customers please allow 20p for postage and packing for the first book and 10p per copy for each additional book.